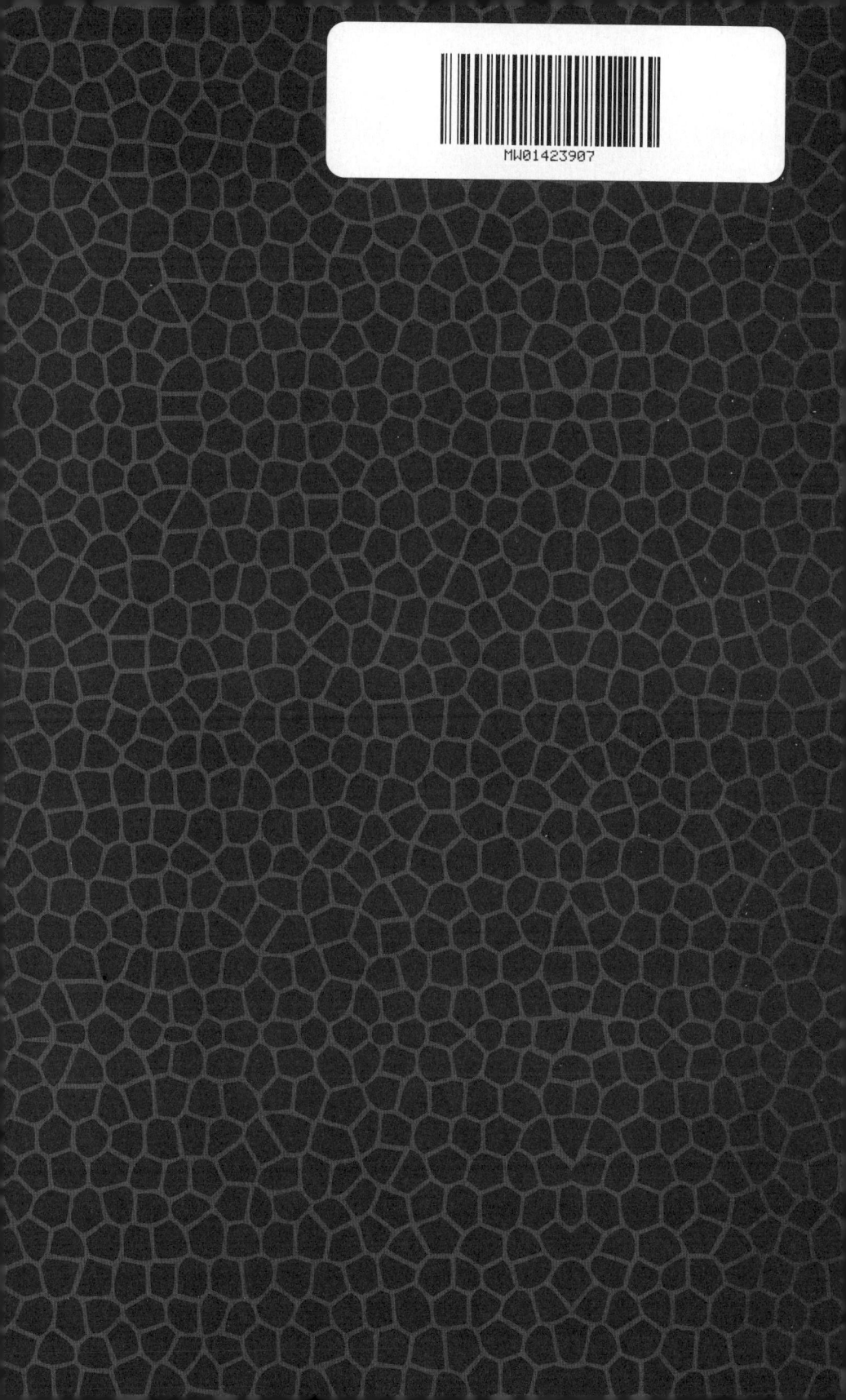

Why Be JEWISH?

MOSAICA PRESS

Why Be JEWISH?

Knowledge and Inspiration for Jews of Today

DORON KORNBLUTH

Copyright © 2011, 2022 by Mosaica Press

ISBN: 978-1-952370-35-9

All rights reserved. No part of this book may be used or reproduced or transmitted in any form or by any means, electronic or mechanical, including photocopying, recording, or by any information storage and retrieval system, without written permission from the publisher.

Published by Mosaica Press, Inc.
www.mosaicapress.com
info@mosaicapress.com

Dedicated in memory of my father

William Mazel, z"l

and in honor of my mother

Irene Mazel

Norfolk, Virginia

Their devotion to Torah, Yiddishkeit, and *chessed* permeated my family and touched countless individuals. Now, their children, grandchildren, and great-grandchildren continue this devotion. It is my hope and prayer that this book rekindles the spark of the Shechinah which resides in every Jewish soul so as to reconnect fellow Jews to their wonderful Torah and heritage.

With *hakaros hatov* to my parents,

JOEL M. MAZEL
COLUMBUS, OHIO
5771/2010

Dedicated to

***Happy Jewish marriages
and families, filled with
love and shalom bayit***

ANONYMOUS

The *Why Be Jewish?* Project
has been sponsored in part by

The Horowitz Family

of Los Angeles, Ca.

The Tabachnick Family

of Pittsburgh, Pa.

and

THE BURD FAMILY

THE EISENSTADT FAMILY

THE GHITTIS FAMILY

THE GLASS FAMILY

THE MOSS-BOKOR FAMILY

THE SHAPERO FAMILY

THE SPINDEL FAMILY

Dedicated to the health and success of

Aaron Eliyahu Valberg

in *gashmius* and especially in *ruchnius*

HIS LOVING PARENTS

Table of Contents

Acknowledgments XIII

Dedication XV
Our Beloved Daniel

Introduction 1

Sundays with Joey 3
A non-Jew's lessons on loyalty—and life

Mandela, Martin, and Me 13
Heroic lessons on tribalism and the universal good

Two Polar Bears in a Bathtub 23
Experiments in going against the flow

Sweet Revenge 29
Birthright's brainwave

Bacon Double Cheese Burger 32
One man's Jewish moment

Library Book 35
Struggles with individualism and destiny

X   *Why Be Jewish?*

Sensing the Supernatural...37
A rationalist's journey

It's the Food..44
Memories of chicken soup and matzah balls

Mendel Rosenbaum..47
Finding God in Block B

Chain of Tradition..49
Who did you receive the tradition from?

The Dalai Lama...57
Surprising advice from the East

May God Bless You, Eric Jones...................................62
Crossing my red lines

United Nations...67
The Jewish vision for the world

Why Stay Jewish...69
Why bother, anyway?

How Many Jews Does It Take to Screw In a Light Bulb?...........72
Lessons from Jewish humor

Love, Jewish Style...77
Judaism's effect on my marriage

Dear Diary..82
Judaism's effect on my family

Community...88
Where everybody knows your name

God Told Me to Be Jewish..93
Indirect directions to stay Jewish

Tolstoy and Me..114
Jewish inspiration from the greatest Russian ever

Appendix I..121
Nobel Prize Winners

Appendix II..135
The Anabasis

Appendix III...137
On Love and Lennon

Acknowledgments

In order to reflect the multiplicity of our Jewish experiences and outlooks, I have taken on different voices within this volume. Some of the voices are old; some are young. Some are male and some are female. The words, unless otherwise indicated, are mine.

But the ideas are not. My thanks go, first and foremost, to the hundreds of students I've taught, and thousands of people I've met over the years in my *Why Be Jewish?* seminars and other classes and lectures. The ideas, reasons, questions, and answers found within these pages belong to them.

Many people shared their insights about this project over the years. My thanks go to all of you for sharing your time and wisdom. Special appreciation goes to Aliza Bulow, Daniel and Lauren Green, Rabbi Yaacov Haber, Judy and Harvey Kornbluth, Mark Kornbluth, Akiva and Rachel Lebowitz, Ari Lieberman and Jack and Joy Siegel.

Rabbi Dov Lev's editing, writing skills, and Jewish wisdom helped improve this work significantly, and his contribution is not to be underestimated.

Mosaica Press has proven to be a perfect fit. I look forward to publishing under the Mosaica label for many years to come.

Several individuals and families have made this project possible. Many of their names are listed in the dedications. I want to take this opportunity to personally thank them for being my partners. Together, we are trying to keep Jews Jewish.

Writing this book was a long process. Deepest thanks to my parents and in-laws for their support, to my children for being so wonderful, and to my wife for believing in me and standing with me throughout all the hard work.

Doron Kornbluth, February 2011
doronkornbluth@gmail.com

Dedication
Our Beloved Daniel

Tuly and Sheryl Wultz

We imagine that if our beloved son, Daniel, had lived beyond his teenage years he would actively contribute to the same mission that inspires the writing and lectures of Doron Kornbluth.

Daniel did not have that opportunity. He was fatally wounded in a suicide bombing at a Tel Aviv restaurant during a family visit to Israel over Passover, 2006. Despite near heroic efforts by his doctors, Daniel's valiant efforts to live ended four weeks later.

Daniel was 16 years old.

It is apropos that this book is published in Daniel's memory. Once you know even a little about the beautiful son we were privileged to raise for 16 years, you will understand.

Daniel was our second child, born almost three years after a daughter whose confidence, strength, intellect, and natural charm from the earliest moments of her life first taught us that being a parent is God's most precious gift.

When Daniel was born and immediately slept through the night after just a few short days at home, we thought we had been doubly blessed with two children who would make parenting an easy task.

Very quickly we discovered that while Daniel brought many gifts to both us, our family, and many others, being a mellow, easy child would not be one of them. Those quiet initial nights turned out to be Daniel storing up mountains of energy that would emerge almost uninterrupted through infancy, childhood, and well into adolescence.

Along with that energy—behind the biggest smile and most loving heart we could have ever imagined—came a bright light and immense embrace of God, family and life itself that continues to touch and inspire us to this day.

Above all else, Daniel loved people, beginning with his family and friends.

Whether he was coming or going to school, preparing for Shabbat, or simply seeing us after a basketball game, Daniel always reached out with the warmest of hugs that even today, nearly five years since our last embrace, continue to bring us strength and comfort.

As he loved his family, Daniel also loved Israel. When we arrived in Israel for the trip that would be our last together, his first words were, "I'm glad to be home."

During that trip, Daniel begged us to let him finish his remaining two years of high school in Israel, not wanting to let even another moment pass before he could begin building his life in the Jewish State.

There were many reasons Daniel loved Israel. From his first interactions, he felt a strong bond with his grandparents, aunts, uncles and cousins who live there. They were always warm, nurturing and loving. Daniel also felt a strong and deep connection with the land. He truly believed that "Am Israel Chai"—the Jewish People are alive!

Daniel's pride and love for Judaism included a deep sense of humility and deep respect for the values and beliefs of others. Daniel's ability to respect others enabled him to reach out and be accepted by young and old, black and white, Jewish and non-Jewish. No one disliked him—he had the rare ability to make friends with all, and thereby, in his way, positively influence those around him. Daniel was mature well beyond his years. When Daniel was about 14 years old he went away to a basketball camp for one week. After the first day he called home to say that his $50 was missing from his wallet. When we said we would speak to the camp director, he asked us not to, saying that whoever took it must really need it. For Daniel, loving Judaism, Israel, his family and all people was the most natural expression of the values that guided his life.

Daniel never spoke badly of others. This value was so important to him that if he heard others speaking negatively about their peers, he would actively reach out to encourage them to stop. He was never shy about phoning a classmate he felt needed a friend, kind word, or someone who would listen. Also, he was never afraid to stand up and do the right thing even when he found himself alone. His commitment to doing good and standing for justice included refusing to be intimidated by the threats and actions of bullies at school, even when they tried to hurt him.

Over the last year and a half of his life, in true "Daniel Style," our son became increasingly observant of Jewish tradition. This decision came with compassion, inner strength, and many, many questions. He kept the phone numbers of his two revered rabbis stored in his cell phone's speed dial and never hesitated to call with a question.

Daniel's love and passions were regularly expressed through tangible acts. He wouldn't consider missing a family gathering even in celebrations at restaurants that weren't kosher. Without making anyone feel awkward, insulted, or sorry for him, he would arrive with a snack to be sure he could keep his commitment to loving his family while also following the religious beliefs he deeply respected.

Family came first.

Not a day passes when we don't miss Daniel's physical presence, warmth, and zest for life. While our 16 years together left us with many cherished moments and memories, his absence left a void in our hearts that will be there for the rest of our lives.

XVIII Why Be Jewish?

Since we last felt Daniel's hand within our own or the loving heart pressed against ours with each embrace, we ask, "Why?" As we witnessed his classmates' high school graduation, we imagined Daniel there, too. As many left to begin their college studies, we imagined the conversations, stories, and experiences that would have been part of our years with Daniel. And as we welcomed our third child into the world, a son born just a week before what would have been Daniel's 18th birthday, we imagined the pure joy and delight with which Daniel would have welcomed his little brother into the world and our family. In fact, Daniel often asked for a younger sibling. Before our last trip to Israel, Daniel remarked that we would have another son. Although Daniel was undeterred, we told him we didn't think that would happen.

We've been grateful for the outpouring of support from people around the world who prayed for Daniel and our family during the weeks he fought to survive. Daniel's memory and the values he taught us gave us strength to continue encouraging the passions we know would have remained central to his life through the Daniel Cantor Wultz Foundation (*www.dcwfoundation.org*), a nonprofit organization for promoting tolerance and acceptance through education and sports initiatives that has touched the lives of many thousands.

We regularly feel Daniel's presence and the quest for answers from God that surely continues in his spirit.

Daniel would have been proud of this important book and honored to help promote the values woven throughout its pages. His life remains a lesson of compassion, faith, strength, and love—building blocks that have sustained our People from time immemorial.

We hope you will find meaning and inspiration from the lessons Doron shares in the pages that follow. In true "Daniel Style," we trust you will find answers to your own questions to guide your heart, spirit and faith through all the days of your life.

Daniel inspired us for a lifetime, teaching us much about the importance and meaning of being Jewish. We were blessed to have Daniel for our son.

Daniel Naftali Meir | 8 Kislev 5750–16 Iyar 5766

Introduction

I spend much of my time speaking to and with Jewish teens, college students, and twenty-somethings. I used to teach Talmud as well as Jewish philosophy and law.

Over the years, my focus has changed. The questions are becoming more basic. Young Jews want to know why they should stay Jewish.

Through most of Jewish history, people never—or at least, rarely—asked this question. Historically, Jews were Jews...because that is what they were. For most of our history, there was no realistic escape from the 'Jewish Condition'—and so our identity was usually accepted for what it was.

But times have changed. More and more Jews see their Jewish identities as a lifestyle choice. They can choose to "opt-in" to Jewish identity. Or, actively or passively, they can step away from their Jewish heritage.

Intelligent and well-intentioned Jews today are asking *why* they should remain Jewish and wondering what it offers them—and the world.

This book is the beginning of my answer.

How to Read This Book

Some books need to be read cover to cover. Some books need to be studied.

This volume can be read any way you prefer. The order is not particularly important. Neither is the pace. Each of its chapters is independent of the others. In each one, I take on a different role. Sometimes I am old, sometimes young. Sometimes male, sometimes female. Skim through, find something that piques your interest, and give it a try. I hope you'll read another and another...

While the pieces seem unrelated to each other, at a deeper level they are very much interconnected. Modern Jews often lack clarity on *why* they are Jewish.

What does our Jewishness offer us, and the world?

How does my Jewish identity fit in with my other definitions (American. British. Israeli. Male. Female. Vegetarian. Mets fan. Democrat. Republican...)?

Is it important to remain Jewish?

Why? What is it all about?

Each chapter of *Why Be Jewish?* is a piece of a puzzle, offering answers to these and other questions. In one essay, I tackle the thorny issue of being committed to one's "tribe" versus the good of the world. In another, I discuss Jewishness and family life. In others, the topics include spirituality, Jewish humor and food, destiny, and fascinating non-Jewish views of Jewishness. Each of us connects to our Jewishness in a particular way. There is no one reason "to be Jewish." Find your own entry point, explore, and get inspired.

Sundays with Joey
A non-Jew's lessons on loyalty—and life

"Look how the brakes are worn down. Not normal wear and tear. Then the rim would be smooth. On this one, there are all these little bumps. Know what makes them? Slamming on the brakes. And not just once. Every day like that. No wonder they didn't last. This is your first lesson of the day: Some people misuse what they have and are later surprised that they don't have it anymore."

I loved spending my Sundays with Joey. My dad and Joey were good friends, even though Joey was thirty years older.

My parents moved into town before I was born, so I don't have any memories of our arrival. But as I understand the story, Joey was the first one to welcome them and make them feel comfortable.

Whenever someone would say something bad about the Jews—which I don't think was often—Joey would stand up for us: "Why, in my Bible it says that Abraham was a Jew and King David was a Jew and Moses was a Jew. Sounds like pretty good folks to me. And my neighbor, Mr. Friedman—why, them is some of the best people in town and you know it as well as I do."

And my dad felt the same way about Joey. "A fine man, he is. Very fine. If only more people were like Joey, the world would be a much better place," I heard him say on more than one occasion.

Joey was like a substitute grandfather for me, since mine were killed in the war. And I was like a substitute grandchild for him, since his kids had moved far away with their families. We needed each other.

Joey was the town mechanic. He knew everything about cars, trucks, motorcycles—he had been fixing them and rebuilding them for as long as anyone could remember.

I'm not sure exactly how it started, but I liked spending time with him and he liked having me around, and my parents liked his influence on me, so I became his student. Joey and his wife would go to church on Sunday morning, go home for lunch, and then he'd drop by to pick me up and we'd go to his garage for the afternoon. He would teach me about fixing cars, and life. Then at 7 p.m., I'd go home and have dinner with my folks.

His lessons about engines stood me well—I rarely need a mechanic these days. And his lessons about life have helped me even more.

As I got older, I understood more about who Joey was. Where his family was from. The good jobs his kids moved away for. What it means to be an American. What it means to be a man. In retrospect, I realize now that Joey—church-going Christian Joey—also taught me about being a Jew.

"Did You Ask Your Folks?"

Being the only Jewish kid in a small town wasn't easy. Sure, it can make you stronger, less able to be passive about things, blah blah blah. That is sometimes true. But usually it goes in the other direction.

And in any case, at the time, when you are a kid, the philosophy doesn't help much. You want to be like the other kids around you. And my friends would spend Monday talking about what fun things they did in the church youth activities on Sunday while their parents were upstairs listening to the sermon.

So I asked Joey if I could come with him to church, "just to see what it is like, and to hang out with the other kids." Joey stopped working on the car and was quiet for what seemed like an eternity. He slowly wheeled out from under the hood and laid his tools on the floor. Just lay there and looked at me long and hard.

"Did you ask your folks?" he asked.

"N-no," I stammered a reply.

"Good. Don't. You'll break their hearts."

"I just wanted to go once, to see…"

"Don't. Going to church is a fine thing for me. But not for you. I know you don't have a synagogue here, and don't have any Jewish friends your age. That must be hard. But church ain't for you. You're a Jew and that is a thing to be proud of. Respect your parents and your religion. Don't you forget that. Now pass me that size 2 and shine some light down here…"

When Joey wanted to end the conversation, he would ask me to pass him a tool and start talking about engines again. End of discussion. And end of my church experience.

Honesty Is the Best Policy

Sometimes I told Joey about things that happened to me during the week. Sometimes he would ask me questions. But sometimes, Joey just seemed to know. There were things he would say that fit exactly with what I was going through. Did he have some Divine insight into what I needed to hear?

I didn't like studying French. But the State said you need four years of language to graduate and Miss Geroux was the only foreign-language teacher in our town, so French it was. Not that anyone could actually speak the language "après" graduation, but those were the rules.

So I procrastinated and didn't study for the final test and failed. I know what you're thinking. Good kid. Does well overall. One test. Big deal. I could still redo the test over the summer and pass the course.

The only problem was my parents. They needed me to be in the store for the summer and now I would need to spend the better part of the next two weeks studying for the test. More importantly, I was their only child. Their hope for the future. How was I going to be a good American if I failed a class? How was I going to succeed if I didn't learn to study things I didn't enjoy? I couldn't tell them—they would be too hurt.

But then how could I get out of the work? And how could I explain my need to study French?

So I lied. I made up a story about extra credit and fewer classes next year. Lying is not atypical for a kid, and I meant well, but still, I lied to my parents. My parents never lied in their lives. Of course they believed me since they never imagined that I would lie to them.

So Sunday afternoon Joey is reassembling an old Ford engine from a pickup truck. It is out there on the table. Big engine. He lifts it out of the truck with a mini-crane he had in the garage just for that purpose. And he is laying out all the parts.

"An engine is like a person's life," he begins.

"See how everything goes in the right place. All these parts fit together perfectly. Each has its rightful place. Not much room for confusion or doubt. Take it apart and I can put it all back again pretty easy. Same thing with life. Someone asks me something and I know what answer to give—the real answer. Because that is the only answer.

"Some people don't know that. They make life more complicated. Say one thing to John and another to Sam and another to Bill. Don't know why—maybe they think people will like them more. Thing is, though, they get found out. Wasn't it President Lincoln who said that liars need a good memory? Who can keep track of anything when you lie? One lie to one and another to another and soon your whole life is a lie.

"Better to see life like an engine. Everything only has one place—its true place. Like this piston—see where it fits in right here….now pass me that wrench."

How did he know? I'm still not sure. But I am sure that I was meant to hear his message that day, sure as he was meant to give it.

Religion Is Like a Garden

Today I am blessed to be a grandfather. And I'm delighted to report that my wife and I have managed to attend every Bar and Bat-mitzvah of our grandchildren so far, wherever around the world they may be.

But it wasn't like that for me growing up. I didn't have any grandparents to come to my Bar Mitzvah. Since I didn't know otherwise, I wasn't particularly disappointed. But it bothered my Dad. So my parents made extra efforts for a special party, made sure to get all the Jewish families we knew from around the State to come, and invited my friends and neighbors.

The surprise guest speaker was Joey.

> *This is my first Bar Mitzvah party and I am enjoying myself very much. I think I'll talk to Reverend Peter about making these for the church kids as well—all with Mrs. Friedman's delicious cakes!*
>
> *So anyway, I wouldn't have missed this for the world, as you all know how I feel about Davie and the family. When Davie's dad invited me to speak, I was really touched. I didn't know what a Bar Mitzvah was, so I went to the library and did some research. Mrs. Pritchard only had one book about Judaism. Thankfully, it had a very nice little chapter on Bar Mitzvahs.*
>
> *What it said there was that this is the day when you change from being a child to a man. Now don't you get cocky and think I'm gonna start paying you for working in the garage, Davie!*
>
> *So you are a man, or at least a young man. But what I read there in the library was that you are not just a man, but that you are now responsible for your actions. You are a 'son of the commandments'—responsible to keep the religion, and the rest...*
>
> *So since your religion is now more in your hands, I want to tell you something and I want all you young folks to listen close. I ain't a preacher and I ain't a rabbi. But I been around and seen a lot of people and I want to tell you something about religion.*
>
> *Religion is like a garden. It needs tending. If you tend your garden, put time and care into it, it will be there for you. It will give you beautiful plants and flowers. You'll feel good about it and be proud of it, as you should be.*
>
> *But if you are lazy about your garden, you'll get weeds and the plants won't grow well. You'll feel bad about it and look away. And others will think badly of it as well.*

> *What I am trying to tell you young folks, is that religion needs tending too. You need to pray. And study. And do whatever you are supposed to do. You'll be happier. And calmer. And nicer. And all that will make you healthier too—just ask Doctor Eugene. And you'll feel good about it and be proud of it. And it will be proud of you.*
>
> *But a man who ignores his religion—because he is lazy or cheap or embarrassed or whatever—he thinks he is saving time. Looking cool. Gaining something. But he isn't. In the end he loses out. A person who doesn't tend the garden can't enjoy the garden. A person who doesn't put into religion won't get much out of it either. Stick by your religion and it'll stick by you. If not...well, a person like that won't have real peace. He won't have real joy. He won't find it easy to talk to God when he really needs that conversation. He didn't sow the seeds and won't be able to reap the harvest.*
>
> *And so now, Davie, you are getting older. You take some responsibility to be a good Jewish person. Like your parents. They are fine folks and I think the world of them. You tend to your religion.*

Everything in Moderation

One Sunday when Joey came over after lunch, my parents told him that I was resting because I wasn't feeling well. I wouldn't be coming over to the garage with him later.

The real reason—which I hid successfully from my parents—was that I had gone to a party the night before and had come home drunk. My first time. I was thus quite hung-over and unable to sit at the table normally or work with Joey at the garage. I told my parents that I wasn't feeling well and they trusted me enough—I guess a little too much—and bought the story hook, line and sinker. They never imagined that a fourteen-year-old boy—their son—would get drunk.

Funny thing is, Joey somehow knew. I think.

You see, other times when I was sick, Joey would stop by to check in on me. But that entire week, he didn't stop in once. Or even call. Strange. Then the next Sunday when he came for lunch, he acted as if everything was normal. Didn't even ask if I was feeling better. Very strange.

A couple of hours later when he was under the hood of the car, he began a story.

> *Did I ever tell you about my friend Woody? He was killed in the war. Nice guy, Woody. From Topeko. My age. We met in boot camp and stuck together. Woody was smarter than I was. Faster. Taller. So it was surprising when I kept getting new bars and stripes and he didn't. Stayed a private his entire stint.*
>
> *Know why? Woody had a fault. He was a man of extremes. He could sprint past me faster than a lion on horseback, but would peter out and come in last in the long runs. He would talk big at the beginning of training and impress everybody—taking all the jobs, leading the guys, but then he'd fall apart two or three weeks down the road and get lazy. He would be the most charming, charismatic guy one second; but then take offence and get in a fight. Cool, rational, thinking, and planning one day. Then get drunk off his rocker one night and sleep in, showing up late and hung-over the next day for roll call and getting us all in the dock.*
>
> *A man of extremes, Woody. Didn't know the value of moderation. How to plan for the long haul. How to enjoy without going over the top. Poor Woody. Never had a chance to learn.*
>
> *He died how he lived—foolishly. Ran ahead too fast while we were advancing without backup. Shot through the mouth, the poor fool. Never learned that sometimes it is best to jog, not run. To have one drink not five. To live a life of moderation. Poor Woody.*
>
> *Now take a look at this valve...*

10 *Why Be Jewish?*

How did Joey know? Was it just a coincidence? Did we have some kind of cosmic connection so that he said what I needed to hear when I needed to hear it?

Live Off the Interest; Don't Touch the Principal

The biggest baseball game of the year was coming up. Not only did the whole high school attend, but practically the whole town did. Everyone in my class would be there. It had been the subject of conversation for weeks. I was excited.

Until I looked at the calendar. The game was on the first day of Rosh Hashana. We were going to be in town for the holidays that year, with a few families from surrounding towns getting together and camping out at our house. My idea was to say the prayers quickly on my own, walk over for the game, and make it back in time for Shofar.

My parents said no.

I tried arguing but my parents didn't want to listen anymore. I spent the next Sunday complaining about it to Joey. Joey answered with a story:

> Did I ever tell you about the man with the million dollars? I once knew a man a little younger than me. Lived in Barleyside, by the river. Normal guy. Normal house. Normal parents. Dad ran a little store. Mom raised the kids. Anyhoo, his parents died when he was in his late twenties and then a couple of years later, when he was thirty, he got a letter from a lawyer type. Inheritance from someone or other.
>
> Million dollars. And I mean a million then was a heck of a lot more than a million now. Anyhoo. So the way things worked out, this guy could leave the million in the bank and live off the interest. Plenty of money. More than he needed. Could be happy, enjoy life, and relax.
>
> But still a pretty normal life. Wouldn't be trotting around the world like a rich guy, sailing on yachts and drinking fine wines. So this guy thought he was bright. And he figured that $900,000 in the bank was still pretty darn good. The

extra would let him live the high life. And we only got one life, right? So he took out $100,000 for fun.

But of course, it wasn't a year or two more until he wanted the high life again. So he took a little more away. And a little more and a little more. Sooner than he realized, his yearly interest was getting lower also—because he was taking away the principal, of course—and so he needed to take even more away, just to break even if you know what I mean. Without the high life.

To make a long story short, he used up the cash before he was 45. Could've lasted a lifetime. But he kept taking away bit by bit until there was nothing left. His mistake was the first $100,000. Once you start taking away bits, where does it end? Yup, that's the way it goes. You tell yourself that it is just this once. But once you start, there it goes. Religion is the same, I say. Once you start skipping the New Year once, why, there doesn't seem like no reason not to skip it again...Like a woman on a diet. Once she eats one piece, she's done gone eating half the cake, if you know what I mean. Don't tell Mrs. Joey I said that, young fellow. She'll take it wrong. Now you pass me that thingamahoo on the table...

Mrs. Joey

I called her Mrs. Joey, and she loved it. She knew the caliber of man she had been married to for forty-five years and was delighted to be reminded of it—especially in such an endearing way.

When Mrs. Joey started to get sick, Joey started going to church more. It used to be just Sunday mornings, but now he went back on Sunday evenings for the "afternoon sermon" and again on Wednesdays for the "midweek communion."

While I know he was still working many hours a day, at the time it seemed like he spent all of his time at the hospital or in church. Except our Sunday afternoons together. I can only think of once or twice that he missed those.

I once asked him why he was going so much.

"A man needs a religion," Joey said. "Life can be hard. Lots of challenges. Emotion. Stress. Why, I pity the poor folks who don't have religion. What reminds them that they are not alone? What gives them comfort? What reminds them not to get all worked up about the little things in life—what was that word your daddy taught me for small things?"

"*Kleinikeit*," I answered.

"Right, *kleinicky*" Joey repeated. He loved Yiddish, though could never pronounce it right.

"What reminds them about the Kingdom of Heaven? How do they get old and not get depressed?"

Goodbye, Joey

I was sixteen when Joey died, and I was devastated. He had a heart attack and was not doing well. Who were the first people Mrs. Joey called? My folks. My mother got on the phone, calling Joey's relatives around the country, the local pastor, and anyone else who needed to know. My dad rushed to the hospital and started filling out paperwork—Mrs. Joey was too distraught. The nurses tried to stop me from going in the room (he was in intensive care and only family members were allowed). Mrs. Joey heard my voice, stopped crying, stood up with authority, and said simply, "This is our grandson. Let him in."

No one ever argued with Mrs. Joey, especially then. You could hardly see Joey underneath all the tubes. I bent over to him and asked, "Can you hear me, Uncle Joey? It's Davie." He wasn't supposed to talk, but he did anyway. It was hard to hear him, but I put my ear near his mouth to catch every word and pretty much succeeded. He told me to do well in school. To make something of my life. To listen to my parents. He told me to stay true to my religion and my country. He told me that he loved me. Then he looked at Mrs. Joey, smiled a little, and closed his eyes.

Goodbye, Joey.

Mandela, Martin, and Me[1]
Heroic lessons on tribalism and the universal good

Mandela. The name itself evokes memories. Hope. Admiration. Nelson Mandela was one of my heroes growing up. We marched for his release from the jail in which he was cruelly imprisoned. We sang songs and wore buttons with the words "Free Nelson Mandela!" printed on them. He was larger than life.

And deservedly so. Already young, Mandela began his struggle against the evil Apartheid regime in South Africa. At first, he led a movement of non-violence, openly drawing inspiration from Mahatma Gandhi. Later, when white oppression and violence escalated, Mandela and his associates felt that their pacifist movement had gotten nowhere while the brutality was increasing daily. As a "last resort," he formed and led the MK, the Sword of the Nation, directing acts of sabotage against the Apartheid regime (but not targeting civilians) in order to try and force them to negotiate. Captured in 1962, he spent twenty-seven years in jail, including eighteen on Robben Island.

---

[1] I don't agree with everything these individuals stood for. Nevertheless, they can teach us many universal lessons.

Robben Island is South Africa's Alcatraz. It was a harsh island prison host to both common criminals and political prisoners. The island is now a national museum and a popular tourist attraction. I visited recently. One of the highlights is Mandela's cell. It has a sleeping mat against one wall and a pail (which acted as a bathroom) against the other. There are only about three feet (one meter) in between the two. A tiny cell. Windows were only installed much later. For much of Mandela's stay, the prisoners suffered from bitter cold in the winter and burning heat in the summer. They performed hard labor in a quarry nearby. As a political prisoner, the lowest classification, he was allowed two visitors and two letters (heavily censored) a year.

Today, former prisoners guide tourists around the site, telling their own stories and the story of modern South Africa. The South African struggle for freedom became real to me. The brutality of the Apartheid regime became real to me.

Mandela survived the terrible conditions. Incredibly, when released in 1990, he walked out without hate. He possessed great wisdom. He emphasized and insisted on National Reconciliation rather than revenge. He envisioned and described a South Africa where all peoples and colors would live together in peace and respect. Elected President of South Africa in 1994, he remains to this day an icon in his home country, and has gained great fame and respect around the world. He received hundreds of honors and awards, culminating in the Nobel Peace Prize in 1993.

As global minded and universalistic as he was, Nelson Rolihlahla Mandela was also a proud and committed African. He was born in 1918 to the Thembu dynasty of South Africa's Western Cape. His great-grandfather was the king, and many of his relatives were considered royalty. His father was the chief of his town of Mvezo, and later a respected member of the Inkosi's Privy Council. Mandela's mother was the daughter of the leader of the Xhosa tribe. Mandela himself was a leader of the African National Congress. When released in 1991, he declared, "During my lifetime I have dedicated myself to the struggle of the African people…" Many of Mandela's relatives and descendants are royalty in various South African tribes, attempting to continue serving their people.

On the one hand, a universal symbol of freedom, hope, and reconciliation. A role model and hero for the entire world.

On the other hand, a man who was deeply connected to his tribe, his people, his continent, and his traditions.

Martin Luther King, Jr.

Martin Luther King was born in 1929 and assassinated in 1968. He was posthumously awarded the Presidential Medal of Freedom, the Congressional Gold Medal, and many other prizes. Perhaps most notably, in 1964 he became the youngest recipient ever of the Nobel Peace Prize for his leadership in the non-violent struggle against American racism and segregation. He led the Montgomery Bus Boycott, as well as numerous marches and movements for voting rights, desegregation, labor rights, and civil rights. At the massive 1963 March on Washington, he delivered his famous "I Have a Dream" speech. This speech, one of the most influential and often-quoted in US history, appealed to the idealism of America and raised public consciousness of the civil rights movement:

> *And so even though we face the difficulties of today and tomorrow, I still have a dream. It is a dream deeply rooted in the American dream...*
>
> *I have a dream that one day on the red hills of Georgia, the sons of former slaves and the sons of former slave owners will be able to sit down together at the table of brotherhood...*
>
> *And this will be the day—this will be the day when all of God's children will be able to sing with new meaning:*
>
> *"My country, 'tis of thee, sweet land of liberty, of thee I sing.*
> *Land where my fathers died, land of the Pilgrim's pride,*
> *From every mountainside, let freedom ring!"*
>
> *And if America is to be a great nation, this must become true.*

> And so let freedom ring from the prodigious hilltops of New Hampshire.
>
> Let freedom ring from the mighty mountains of New York.
>
> Let freedom ring from the heightening Alleghenies of Pennsylvania.
>
> Let freedom ring from the snow-capped Rockies of Colorado.
>
> Let freedom ring from the curvaceous slopes of California.
>
> But not only that:
>
> Let freedom ring from Stone Mountain of Georgia.
>
> Let freedom ring from Lookout Mountain of Tennessee.
>
> Let freedom ring from every hill and molehill of Mississippi.
>
> From every mountainside, let freedom ring.
>
> And when this happens, when we allow freedom to ring, when we let it ring from every village and every hamlet, from every state and every city, we will be able to speed up that day when all of God's children, black men and white men, Jews and Gentiles, Protestants and Catholics, will be able to join hands and sing in the words of the old Negro spiritual:
>
> "Free at last! Free at last!
>
> Thank God Almighty, we are free at last!"

Martin Luther King, Jr. was not just a civil rights leader. He was a Baptist preacher, pastor of the Dexter Avenue Baptist Church, and son of the Reverend Martin Luther King, Sr.

Martin Luther King, Jr. was well grounded in the Bible, which had a profound impact on his life. He often used Biblical imagery. In his last speech before being assassinated, referring to threats against his life, he said:

> Well, I don't know what will happen now. We've got some difficult days ahead...But it doesn't matter with me now. Because I've been to the mountaintop. And I don't mind. Like anybody, I would like to live a long life. Longevity has its place.

> But I'm not concerned about that now. I just want to do God's will. And He's allowed me to go up to the mountain. And I've looked over. And I've seen the Promised Land. I may not get there with you. But I want you to know tonight, that we...will get to the Promised Land.

In this passage, King was openly referring to the end of Moses' life, where Moses—though not permitted to enter the Land of Israel—was allowed to climb a mountain and gaze into it.

King was a believing Christian who dedicated his life to the freedom and dignity of African-Americans. And he became a world symbol of freedom and non-violence.

On the one hand, a universal symbol of freedom, hope, and reconciliation. A role model and hero for the entire world.

On the other hand, a man who was first and foremost deeply connected to his religion, his people, and his particular cause.

Agnes Gonxha Bojaxhiu

Born in 1910 in Albania, Agnes Gonxha Bojaxhiu dedicated her life to the poor and suffering in Calcutta, India. Starting alone, by the end of her life her organization (Missionaries of Charity) had more than 4,000 humanitarian centers around the world.

No one was turned away. She cared for the lepers, the untouchables, the orphans, the sick, the dying, the blind, the homeless, refugees, and all other types of suffering people. For decades, she was consistently found by pollsters to be the most widely admired person in the USA, and in a poll in 1999, was found to be the "most admired person of the 20th century." She won many prizes including the Nobel Peace Prize in 1979 for her humanitarian work. She died in 1997 at the age of 87.

Agnes Gonxha Bojaxhiu was a Roman Catholic nun best known as Mother Teresa. At the age of twelve, she felt "the call of God" and decided to be a Christian missionary. At eighteen, she left her parents' home and joined the Sisters of Loretto, taking her vows as a nun and moving to India to teach in a Catholic school in Calcutta, which she did for seventeen years before focusing on the poorest of the poor. She was a deeply committed Christian who consistently reminded others that God and religion were the driving forces behind her work. Dealing with various communities in India, she said, "I've always said we should help a Hindu become a better Hindu, a Muslim become a better Muslim, a Catholic become a better Catholic..." Her talks and work were strongly religious as was her worldview.

On the one hand, a universal symbol of caring, self-sacrifice, and love. A role model and hero for the entire world.

On the other hand, a woman—a nun—who was deeply connected to her religion, her heritage, and her traditions.

Jamphel Ngawang Lobsang Yeshe Tenzin Gyatso

Gyatso was born into a poor farming family in rural Tibet in 1935, which survived on growing barley, buckwheat, and potatoes. He was the fifth of sixteen children, nine of whom survived infancy.

Tenzin Gyatso has become one of the world's leading voices for non-violence, universal human rights, and religious harmony. His life of dedication to the promotion of these values, tremendous impact on world thought, and the inspiration he has given tens of millions, have led to much international recognition for his work.

As an indication of the great esteem in which his work is held, here are only some of the awards he has received:

In 1989, he received the Raoul Wallenberg Human Rights Award from the Congressional Human Rights Caucus, and Le Prix de la Memoire from the Foundation Danielle Mitterrand.

In 1991, he received the Peace and Unity Awards from the National Peace Conference, the Earth Prize from the United Earth and U.N. Environmental Program, and the Advancing Human Liberty award from the Freedom House.

In 1994, he received the Roosevelt Four Freedoms Award from the Franklin and Eleanor Roosevelt Institute, the World Security Annual Peace Award from the New York Lawyer's Alliance, and the Berkeley Medal from University of California, Berkeley.

In 1999, he received the Life Achievement Award from Hadassah Women's Zionist Organization.

In 2003, he received the Jaime Brunet Prize for Human Rights, the Hilton Humanitarian Award, and the International League for Human Rights Award.

In 2006, he received honorary Canadian citizenship and, in 2007, the United States Congressional Gold Medal.

Most famously, he was awarded the Nobel Peace Prize in 1989 for his great service to mankind, in which he "has come forward with constructive and forward-looking proposals for the solution of international conflicts, human rights issues, and global environmental problems."

Never heard of him?

Tenzin Gyatso is better known as the 14th Dalai Lama. He is the world's most famous Buddhist monk and leader (in exile) of the Tibetan government, now residing in Dharamsala, India. Identified at the age of two as the reincarnation of his predecessor, the 13th Dalai Lama, he began his Buddhist education and eventually received his Doctorate in Buddhist philosophy. At the age of fifteen, in 1950, he was enthroned as Tibet's absolute ruler, in both spiritual and political matters. With the Chinese invasion and occupation of Tibet, he has spent almost his entire lifetime trying to rally pressure against China to stop its aggression of the Tibetan culture, language, and population. He eventually was forced to flee Tibet as he suspected that the Chinese government was trying to kill him. The Dalai Lama then established the Tibetan Government in Exile, created schools, monasteries, convents, and programs to preserve and promote Tibetan culture and education.

On the one hand, a universal symbol of harmony, peace, and hope. A role model and hero for the entire world.

On the other hand, a man who has dedicated his life to the freedom, autonomy, and cultural survival of his people, country, and religious traditions.

Mahatma Gandhi

Born in 1869 in what was then British India, Mahatma Gandhi trained as a lawyer and became active in the South African Indian community's struggle for civil rights. He founded the Natal Indian Congress in 1894 and thus molded the Indian community of South Africa into a strong political force. His social activism increased upon his return to India, where he organized the working poor to protest against both oppressive taxation and widespread discrimination. He became the leader of the Indian National Congress, and led nationwide campaigns against poverty, caste discrimination, and ethnic strife, and led his people towards economic self-sufficiency and independence.

He was imprisoned many times for many years in both South Africa and India. In 1930, Gandhi led over 100,000 Indians in a famous "Salt March" to protest cruel British taxation policies, the most famous example of his non-violent strategy of opposing foreign rule. His non-violent approach to social and political change became a model for the American Civil Rights movement and many other similar movements around the world.

One of the most recognized and admired figures of the twentieth century, Gandhi received many prizes and awards. Interestingly, though nominated five times, he was never actually awarded the Nobel Prize (the Executive Director for the Nobel Foundation Michael Sohlam has said publicly that this omission was "a big regret" of the Nobel Foundation).

Gandhi advocated non-violence in all situations without exception. He lived very simply, making his own clothes and living on a simple vegetarian diet. He would often fast for long periods of time, originally for self-purification and later as a method of protest as well. Gandhi was both a student and teacher of Hindu philosophy.

On the one hand, a universal symbol of peace, non-violence, and humility. A role model and hero for the entire world.

On the other hand, a fervent Hindu who dedicated his life to his people, his cause, and his country.

Elie Wiesel

Born in Sighet, Romania, in 1928, Elie Wiesel's family members were observant Jews of Chassidic background. His grandfather was a farmer. His father was a shopkeeper who was imprisoned for several months for helping Polish Jews who escaped to Hungary in the early years of World War II. Most of his family was murdered in the Holocaust, and

Wiesel vividly describes his own experiences in his many novels and works on the Holocaust.

The Nobel Committee awarded him the Nobel Peace Prize in 1986, calling him a "messenger to mankind," who had struggled with "his own personal experience of total humiliation and of the utter contempt for humanity shown in Hitler's death camps," and worked hard for peace, thus offering a powerful message of "peace, atonement, and human dignity."

Aside from teaching about the Holocaust, he has advocated for Israel's right to self-defense, victims of apartheid in South Africa, Argentina's Desaparecidos, Bosnian victims of genocide in the former Yugoslavia, Nicaragua's Miskito Indians, and the Kurds. He recently voiced support and became active on behalf of international intervention in Darfur, Sudan.

On the one hand, a universal symbol of survival, dignity, and human rights activism. A role model and hero for the entire world.

On the other hand, a committed Jew, deeply connected to his religion, his heritage, and his People.

Solving the Contradiction

Does a person need to choose between commitment to one's own people versus a more general focus on universal betterment?

In reality, there is no choice to be made. Time and time again, in these famous examples and thousands more of less famous ones, we find a surprising pattern. Those who did and do great things for the world seem to do so from within their dedication to their own religion, culture, and identity.

Elie Wiesel, Nobel Prize winner and champion of universal human rights, spoke clearly of the connection between his own Jewish identity and his service to the world:

> Remember: the Jew influences his environment only if he does not assimilate. Others will benefit from his experience to the degree that it is and remains unique. Only by assuming his Jewishness can he attain universality. The Jew who

repudiates himself, claiming to do so for the sake of humanity, will inevitably repudiate humanity too...

By working for his own People, a Jew does not renounce his loyalty to mankind. On the contrary, he makes his most valuable contribution...By struggling on behalf of Russian, Arab, or Polish Jews, I fight for human rights everywhere. By calling for peace in the Middle East, I take a stand against every aggression, every war. By protesting the fanatical exhortations to "holy wars" against my People, I protest the stifling of freedom [in general]...By striving to keep alive the memory of the Holocaust, I denounce the massacres in Biafra...

Only by drawing on his unique experience can the Jew help others. A Jew fulfills his role as man only from inside his Jewishness.[2]

As the great sage, Hillel put it two thousand years ago:

If I am not for myself, who will be for me?

If I am only for myself, what am I?

And if not now, when?

Being committed to one's Jewish identity does not come at the expense of one's universal vision. It is a vital element of that vision.

---

2   Elie Wiesel, *"Pride in Being Jewish"* quoted in Dov Peretz Elkins, *Loving My Jewishness*, p. 19.

Two Polar Bears in a Bathtub
Experiments in going against the flow

I was in eighth grade and my classmate Kevin came over to me. He told me to sit down because he had a great joke to tell me. A few of the guys were smiling.

> *Two polar bears are sitting in a bathtub. The first one says, "Pass the soap."*
>
> *One of the onlookers started cracking up and holding his stomach. As he left our little group, he kept laughing and repeating the words, "I can't, I can't..."*

Kevin looks at me and finishes the joke.

> *So again, two polar bears are sitting in a bathtub. The first one says, "Pass the soap." And then...the second one says...[here Kevin had to hold himself in]...the second one says, "No soap, radio!"*

At this point, the entire group gathered around started losing it. I don't mean little chuckles or a chortle or two. I mean sidesplitting guffaws. Loud, uproarious belly laughter.

I was the only person not laughing. I was the only person who didn't get the joke. They were starting to notice. So I started laughing too.

This made everyone else laugh even more. Only much, much later did I realize why.

Kevin and the guys had set me up with a non-joke, a punch line lacking any humor at all. They planned and faked the laughing. The whole point was to put me on the spot. They wanted to see if I would laugh along with the group just to fit in, despite having nothing funny to laugh at.

There was no joke, except on me. And I fell for it.

The Asch Paradigm

A more scientific version of the now-famous "No Soap, Radio" joke was conducted by psychologist Solomon Asch. His experiments, published in 1953, have become famous for demonstrating the amazing power of conformity in groups.

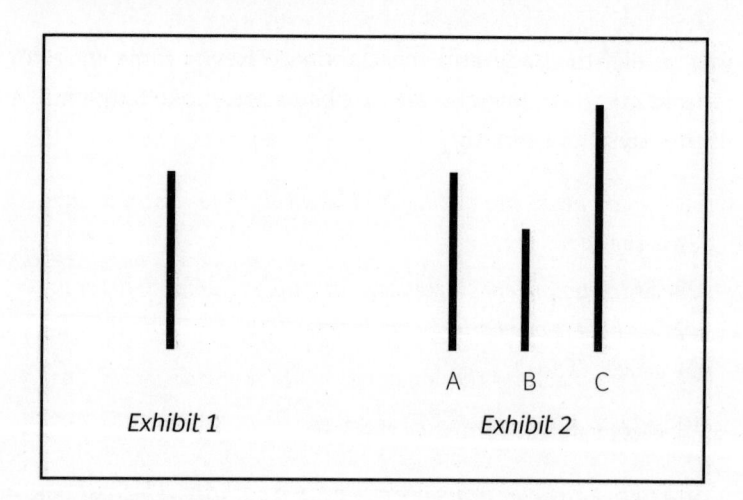

Exhibit 1   A   B   C
Exhibit 2

Groups of eight students were invited to participate in vision tests. They were to look at two cards. One card had three lines of varying lengths. The other had one line, which matched the length of one of the lines on the other card. The stated goal was to check students' vision and ask them to identify which of the three lines matched the length of the line on the other card. The differences in line length were both significant and obvious.

In truth, all of the participating students—with one exception in each session—were "in on the joke." The "fake" students would, by prior agreement, give wrong answers and identify the wrong line. Dr. Asch was not interested in testing students' vision. The goal was to see how the one "real" test participant would react: would he stand up for what his eyes clearly told him? Or would he change his answer in order to avoid sticking out and looking foolish?

The results were astounding. Seventy-five percent agreed with the incorrect answers at least once. The more "fake" participants there were, the higher the proportion of incorrect answers given by the "real" participant. The more uniform the "fake" participants were in their incorrect answers, the higher the proportion of incorrect answers given by the "real" participant.

Dr. Asch's experiments taught that in order to avoid standing out, a large percentage of people will go along with an incorrect majority, even when the majority's mistake seems very obvious.

A question always lingered about the Asch Paradigm, though. Did the "real" participants choose to lie to avoid potential embarrassment, or did they somehow come to really agree with the "fake" participants' (incorrect) answers?

In 2005, Dr. Gregory Berns, a neuroscientist from Emory University in Atlanta, conducted Asch-type experiments while monitoring the brain's activity using M.R.I. scanners. His findings were later published in the Biological Psychiatry Journal.

Dr. Berns' approach was based on an amazing realization. If subjects were consciously lying, the M.R.I. should show activity and change in the frontal areas of the brain that deal with conscious decision-making and conflict resolution. If, on the other hand, the subjects somehow came to believe the group's (incorrect) answers, activity and changes should appear in the back areas of the brain that deal with vision and objective spatial perception.

Confirming the Asch paradigm once again, Dr. Berns and his team found that "real" participants often agreed with the group's obviously incorrect answers.

The M.R.I. scans were even more revealing. Scans of "real" participants who conformed to the group's incorrect answers revealed activity in areas of the brain devoted to vision and objective perception. No activity was recorded in areas devoted to decision-making and conflict resolution.

In other words, when faced with a majority opinion that is clearly contrary to physical reality, *almost half of the population will not only go along with the majority, but will come to actually believe that the majority is right.*

Nineteen Eighty-Four

This idea was perhaps brought out best in George Orwell's *Nineteen Eighty-Four*. This novel, one of the classics of modern literature, is a devastating critique of totalitarianism. It tells the story of Winston Smith who lives in a fictional future society where "Big Brother" is constantly watching. In the story, the state wants full control of its citizens, including their thoughts and opinions. When Smith begins to question the State's monopoly on truth, he is eventually arrested. Ultimately, under the threat of torture, he accepts the State's motto that "2 + 2 = 5," symbolizing his complete surrender to group-think, despite his own prior knowledge of how ridiculous their version of truth is.

Historical parallels of group-think and state-think are all too common. Nazi Reichsmarschall Hermann Göring once demonstrated his loyalty to Adolf Hitler by declaring that, "If the Führer wants it, two and two makes five!"[1] Long ago, Chinese administrator Zhao Gao devised an original loyalty test. He brought a deer into a government chamber and called it a horse. Officials who would agree (to point at a deer and call it a horse) lived. Those who showed independent thought did not. Many more examples exist throughout history.

Swimming Upstream

It is understandable, and most human, to prefer going along with the flow. Nobody wants to stand out. It is lonely. It is uncomfortable.

---

[1] From Wikipedia, "2 + 2 = 5".

Occasionally, it can be dangerous. There is safety in numbers. And comfort. Life isn't easy. Why make it harder by disagreeing with the majority?

On the other hand, sometimes the Emperor really has no clothes.

Going along with the majority is problematic because of its inherent falsehood. Furthermore, it also leads down a terrible path. Societal norms have often caused terrible tragedies. Majorities in many societies of the past practiced human sacrifice. The ancient Greeks practiced infanticide if the baby was deformed, dull, or, often, female. The ancient Romans' favorite societal pastime was watching starved animals, or gladiators, attack, maim, and kill innocent women and children whose great offense was being born in foreign lands. More recently, Hitler was elected in a democratic election by the German electorate. And terrorists enjoy wide support in certain countries. Is the majority always right?

Tool of Resistance

Abraham was a "Hebrew," an English version of the Bible's "Ivri," which refers to the fact that he was *"oh-ver"*—he had crossed to the other side. He stood on one side of a great philosophical debate (monotheism versus idolatry) and held his ground even though the whole world was on the other side. We are a nation of Hebrews—we stand up for truth. Russian anthropologist Michael Chlenov perhaps put it best when he wrote that, "Judaism is a tool of resistance." Throughout history, the presence of a distinct Jewish community has always been a clear challenge to absolutist claims and majority rule.

The Assyrians worshipped idols and bid us to do the same. We refused and, directly and indirectly, reminded the world that the Assyrian view was not the only way of understanding life.

The Greeks admired the human body above all else, while we taught that the soul is supreme.

Roman society was brutal (gladiators versus innocent men and women) and shockingly sexualized (pedophilia was widely practiced). We were examples of kindness and monogamy.

Christianity believes that God had a child, who was also 'part of God,' and later died on the cross for our sins. Throughout the centuries, Jews rejected these claims and answered that God cannot be born, die, or mate, and that each individual needs to improve themselves in order to repair the wrongs they've done—no one can do it for us.

Throughout history, our commitment to our beliefs has challenged the conventional wisdom. This has often provoked no little antagonism. Yet being Jewish has done the world a great service. We have stood firm against the winds. We have taken a stand. We have opposed and continue to oppose idol worship, rampant materialism, and consumerism. We resist the path of least resistance. The easy way. We reject falsehood, evil, and immorality.

Being Jewish is a wonderful privilege and opportunity. It means being committed to seeking the truth. To admiring and developing knowledge and wisdom. It means focusing on a better future, the Messianic Age, and working towards it. It means standing up against the world's false gods—whatever they may be in any given generation—and standing up for the truth.

Sweet Revenge
Birthright's brainwave

I was born in 1983 and grew up in northern California. My mom is Jewish. I never knew my biological father. While most of the time we were a mother/daughter family, mom remarried a few times (it is, after all, California). None of the "father figures" in my life were Jewish. To be honest, the lack of Jewish connections never seemed to matter. We weren't Christian. We weren't anything, really. Free spirits. A little New Age. Somewhat Buddhist, depending on my mom's mood at the time.

I was raised to love everyone. Including animals. And Mother Earth.

I decided to go to UC Santa Cruz because of the trees. I'm serious. It is a beautiful campus lodged in the middle of an enchanting forest. The students' gym was constructed to look out over the ocean, so you have a great view while you jog. That is how I chose the location of my higher education.

When I walked past the student union building and a rabbi asked me, "Are you Jewish?" I said yes. To be honest, I would've said yes if he had asked me if I was Buddhist, New Age, Sufi, searching, or many other labels. He offered me a free trip to Israel, as part of Birthright. I'd heard of Birthright but never really considered it. Too busy walking in the trees. But as I listened to his description, I thought to myself, why not? I had nothing special going on during the dates he mentioned. Ten Days. Free. Happy Grandmother. Why not, indeed?

The trip was awesome. Fun. Interesting. Non-stop. And surprisingly deep. There weren't many classes on Judaism, but the guide would share ideas and keep me thirsting for more.

Growing up with meditation, I never really understood the attraction of formal prayer until I saw it at the Western Wall. The people I saw were as connected as anything I'd ever felt. No wonder. The whole country was magic. There was a form of spirituality around that I'd never imagined—one that was deeply involved in daily life.

And I started to feel more. I felt a connection to these people. To *my* people. They regarded me as one of their own, and the feelings were reciprocated. Old ladies would stop me on the street and ask if I was eating enough. Half the country was my Jewish grandmother.

Towards the end of the trip, we visited the Ghetto Fighters' Museum and met with a Holocaust survivor. She told us her story. What happened to her. And her family. The cruelty. The terror. The incredible miracles that allowed her to survive. How she rebuilt her life. Of course, I knew about the Holocaust, but I'd never met a survivor before. I cried during her entire talk. She was persecuted and tortured because she was Jewish. And it could have happened to me as well.

At the end of her talk, she said something that has stuck with me ever since:

> *I am speaking to you today for two reasons. I am here for you and for me. For you, it is vital that you know what happened. Read about it. Understand it. And meet survivors. Already in my lifetime, they are denying it. It will get worse when we are all gone.*
>
> *That is the first reason. But I also come for myself. Because seeing you here makes me happy. I see you coming to Israel. Coming to learn about your heritage and your religion. Trying to make Jewish friends. Trying to stay Jewish.*
>
> *They wanted us all dead. Men, women, and children. They wanted our religion dead, too. By visiting Israel, you are beating*

the Nazis. By staying Jewish, you are beating the Nazis. You, sweet children, are my sweet revenge.

That phrase has stuck with me. Sweet revenge. I feel more Jewish now than ever. And I owe it to Birthright.

Bacon Double Cheese Burger
One man's Jewish moment

Nice guy, my doctor. Top medical school. Knows what he is doing and answers whatever questions you have. I like him.

Still, I try to avoid him whenever I can. Nothing personal. I'm just not great with medical stuff. I hate tests. I hate the questions. I hate the guilt. My attitude has always been, "I'm overweight, overstressed, don't exercise, and couldn't tell a protein from a pre-teen—just leave me alone, okay?"

If I have a specific problem, I'll go. But otherwise, I know what he is going to say and also know that I'm not going to change. So why bother wasting time and money by visiting him?

So seven years ago, I'm in a McDonalds having a bite to eat for lunch. The doctor's secretary, an African-American woman, walks by me and smiles. She's worked for my doctor for decades and knows all his clients, even the delinquent ones like me.

"Hi, how are you, Mr. Friedman?" she asks politely.

I could have just smiled. Or said, "Good, thank you." Or said, "Good, how are you?"

Instead, I said back, "Good, thanks. When you get back to the office, please tell the doctor that I send my regards, and will arrange for a check-up soon."

I'm not sure why I said it. Likely, I was feeling guilty about ignoring my health and my doctor's advice. But sometimes I think there was more to it—maybe, just maybe, God put the words in my mouth.

Listen to what happened next:

She stands still for a moment, as if thinking about something serious. Then she responds calmly, "I'll pass on the message, but can't do so today—Dr. Rosen is not working today. It is Yom Kippur." She looks at me, looks down at my tray, smiles, and walks away.

Wait, it's not over. Here's the worst part: On my tray is a half-eaten bacon double cheeseburger. I kid you not. On Yom Kippur. Maybe she doesn't know that I'm Jewish? Of course she knows I'm Jewish. I look Jewish. I sound Jewish. I have a Jewish last name. That is exactly why she hesitated—because she knows that I'm Jewish.

I'm sitting in this McDonalds on Yom Kippur eating a bacon double cheeseburger and I have this sudden realization. Everyone knows I'm Jewish, except me. I ignore it, forget it, and eat this, here on Yom Kippur.

I wish I could tell you that I got up, left the restaurant, visited Israel, and vowed to be a good Jew from that moment on.

In truth, though, I finished the burger. I was hungry.

But the whole experience did shake me up. This African-American Christian had more respect for my heritage than I did. I couldn't stop thinking about it.

And wait till you hear this: A few weeks later I'm in the shopping center and see an old school buddy of mine named Mark. Bump into him every couple of years. So we're schmoozing and along comes a big, long beard attached to a rabbi. They smile at each other, shake hands quickly, and Mark introduces me. The rabbi then apologizes to my friend that he is in a rush and says, "See you Tuesday!"

Tuesday? What is Tuesday?

So Mark tells me that every Tuesday a bunch of guys get together at the rabbi's house. They eat, have something to drink, schmooze and the rabbi introduces an idea about life which they then discuss. About marriage. Kids. Work. Being Jewish. Mark tells me he and the guys look forward to it.

So I figure, why not? What else do I do on a Tuesday night? Watch television, read a magazine, and go to sleep. So I go and I am hooked. Gives me something to think about. Good male bonding. Night out. Has improved my marriage and my life. Makes me feel like a Jew.

Since the whole thing started, I have also put more efforts into my Judaism. I surprised my wife with a *menorah* at Chanukah time, which we now light every year. We started going to our cousins' Passover seders again.

A rabbi I am not. But a Jew I am.

Library Book
Struggles with individualism and destiny

Imagine you are in a large room. The largest room you have ever seen. And it is filled with books, millions of books of all colors, shapes, and bindings.

You are not in a rush. You like books and enjoy walking through the stacks, choosing ones that seem interesting, sitting on a chair and reading, getting lost in the thoughts of writers from contemporary times and ages past. You pick up whatever interests you and read it for as long as you want. Once a book loses your interest, you move on to another, leaving the first to be read by someone else or perhaps ignored altogether. Each is just a book, and you have no obligation to start it, finish it, or remember it at all.

An old, leather-bound volume grabs your attention. You are not sure why you are drawn to it. You open the book and are shocked to see your family name at the top of the first page. Intrigued, you start scanning the book. Its subject is your family. Generation by generation, your ancestors tell their story, page after page. The book is filled with amazing individual stories. They tell of who they were, what they did, what struggles they went through, what was important to them, and what they were trying to achieve. Some were rich, some were poor; they spoke various languages and lived in various countries.

But what stands out is that much more than the differences, your family had a remarkable unity and direction. Their traditions and identities were very important to them. This family didn't just live—they were living for something. They lived beautiful lives, and struggled (and, so far, succeeded) in passing on their traditions generation after generation.

A thought comes into your head and you momentarily close the book. Can it be? Dare you look? You hesitate and briefly consider returning the book to its place on the shelf and walking away. But you don't. You know there is no choice but to look at the last entry.

It has your name and date of birth. The rest of the page is blank, clearly waiting for you to describe your part in the family saga.

Part of you rejects the implications of this book and wishes you had never opened it. Generations past cannot obligate you to anything. Their ideals were theirs, not yours. They are gone. You are here. No one can tell you how to lead your life.

But another part of you, the deeper and truer part, knows why you were drawn to this book. In a moment, your life has been changed. Now you understand who you really are. You were not born into a vacuum. You are part of a chain of people who believed in something beautiful, and lived for it. The fulfillment of their lives, hopes, and dreams depends on you.

Will you walk away from the book and its implications? Or will you live and write your chapter and then pass the book onto your children to do their part?[1]

---

1   Based on a story told by Rabbi Jonathan Sacks.

Sensing the Supernatural
A rationalist's journey

George Washington was the first President of the USA. Moscow is the capital of Russia. Dogs have four legs.

These are examples of *outer knowledge*. They are facts that are external to me. They are objective realities. They represent the natural world and reality as we know it. They constitute much, or most, of our knowledge.

But there is a second category of knowledge, *inner knowledge*. I love my wife. Although I demonstrate my love in many ways, I can't really prove it logically. Maybe I'm faking it. Maybe I'm tricking even myself. Maybe I don't even know what love really means.

But it is not so. With a deep, certain and innate knowledge, I know I love her. My love is real. And true. I know it. This is *inner knowledge*.

Attaining Knowledge of God

Belief in God often begins with logic, *outer knowledge*. For example, some people begin questioning: if all the matter in the universe was once condensed into one single point (before exploding in the Big Bang), where did it all originate from—how does something come from nothing? Others may ask, where does morality come from—how is there anything such as right or wrong without God? Still others may ask, how does one explain the incredible enigma of the Jews?

People look at the facts and draw conclusions. There are many books and lectures on the subject of intellectual investigation into the existence of God and the truth of Judaism. This outer knowledge, fact-based path to God is both valid and important.

But it is only the beginning. True knowledge of God is inner knowledge. The logic may have helped me, and is part of my belief, but I also somehow move beyond the logic. My knowledge of Him is logical, but also intuitive. Deep. Profound. Personal. Real. Complete. Inner.

There are many ways to arrive at *outer knowledge*, and they are all important. But how does one come to *inner knowledge?* Often, things just 'fall into place' and 'begin to make sense.' There is, in addition, one method, easily available, that has helped me, and many other people, come to and strengthen their inner knowledge. Let me explain.

My Grandmother

There is an ancient Jewish custom of leading the prayers on the *yahrzeit*, the anniversary of the day of death, of loved ones. My grandmother had passed away and I wanted to lead the prayers on her *yahrzeit* day. I had moved to a small town, which hardly had a *minyan*[1] at all.

There were two problems with my plan to honor my grandmother's memory. First, I am bad with dates. Especially Hebrew ones. I have calendars in my home and office, but still tend to forget things. Often. Second problem, more minor, is that I dread leading the prayers. I don't do it much and I'm not very good at it. Still, I was prepared to overcome my embarrassment and honor my grandmother's memory.

The anniversary of her death was still several weeks away. I decided to attend services once before the *yahrzeit* in order to know what to do when the time came. When I arrived, I was told that the rabbi was out of town and the cantor was sick. The guy who acted as unofficial substitute cantor also wasn't in town. His son, who helped every once in a while, had a bad case of laryngitis and came to say (figuratively

---

1   Prayer quorum.

speaking, of course) that we were on our own. The other people present said that the last time this happened was twenty-three years ago. They made it abundantly clear that they could not possibly lead the prayers. After successfully avoiding it for over a decade, there was no choice. I remember thinking to myself that no matter how bad I was this time, at least I'd be in better shape for the *yahrzeit*. To make a long story short, everything worked out fine. A few days later, when I checked the Jewish calendar, I was shocked to realize that I'd somehow gotten the dates mixed up. Incredibly, I'd lead the prayers on the exact day of her *yahrzeit*.

I randomly chose which day to attend. If any of the regulars had been there, I wouldn't have led the prayers. Several people 'just happened' to be away and others were sick. First time in twenty-three years, there was no one to lead the prayers. Except me, on the very day I needed to.

Buying Our First Home

We were buying our first house. All of our savings, some help from family, and a bank mortgage managed to cover the cost. Or so we thought. What I hadn't properly calculated was the extra expenses that would crop up before we could move in. Fixing the roof. Painting the downstairs. Municipal property tax. Paying the movers. Etc, etc. It added up to almost exactly $15,000. A significant sum in any circumstances, and these weren't normal circumstances. We were already getting the biggest loan that the bank would give. There were no savings left and I already was overloaded on unpaid credit card charges. My wife's parents had passed away and she had no siblings. My family had helped as much as they could, and had even less cash than we did. None of our friends had money to lend.

Even if I had someone who would lend the money, how could I possibly pay it back? We were already overburdened with debt payments. I didn't know what to do. Six weeks of stress didn't lead to a solution. The unpaid bills were piling up and I wasn't sleeping or eating properly. If I wasn't able to pay a significant portion of the bills by next Tuesday, we were in real trouble. I drove to Atlantic City to gamble but only ended up $250.00 more in the hole. My wife sold her jewelry, but all together it was worth less than $1,000.00. Selling our car was a possible option, but it was only worth $1,500.00, and would leave us stranded and unable to get to work.

On Thursday, I got a work bonus of $2,000.00. I had been working there for four years without any bonus at all and I had no idea it was coming. No one at my office knew of our financial bind. No one else got any bonus that year at all.

On Friday, we got a letter from a lawyer that my wife's grandfather's brother left her an inheritance of $9,000. Sadly, there had been fighting between the brothers and the families drifted apart. She hadn't even known he had died. It was the only inheritance either of us ever received, and the timing was literally unbelievable.

On Sunday, close friends who had somehow sensed our situation without ever being informed of it, dropped off an envelope with $3,250 in cash, telling us that we could return it whenever we wanted, even if it took years. Add up $1,000 from the jewelry, $2,000 from the bonus, $9,000 from the inheritance, $3,250 from our friends and you get…$15,250—the exact amount we needed (after I returned from Atlantic City). It got us out of the hole. We were able to keep our home.

Synchronicity

Accounts like this are called by different names. Swiss psychiatrist and thinker Carl Jung called them instances of "synchronicity." Judaism refers to them as examples of *hashgachah pratis*, Divine Providence. Whether one attributes them to fate, destiny, or God, instances of incredible and impossible-to-explain-rationally events are quite common. I like the phrase used in the title of the bestselling book series full of such stories, "Small Miracles."

Some dispute the validity of such stories and, when left with no other choice, claim it is all coincidence. I understand this position, because I used to share it. Until the stories above, and many others, started to happen to me. I looked into many other documented stories and started to rethink my position.

Lincoln and Kennedy

It was during this period that I visited Ripley's Believe It Or Not Museum in Times Square, Manhattan. The famous exhibits are tall people, small people, thin people, and fat people. Huge animals. But there are also exhibits of 'Things to Think About,' including the following facts about U.S. Presidents Abraham Lincoln and John F. Kennedy, who were both famously assassinated:

1. Abraham Lincoln was elected to Congress in 1846. John F. Kennedy was elected to Congress in 1946.
2. Lincoln was elected President in 1860. Kennedy was elected President in 1960.
3. Both men were deeply involved in civil rights for African Americans.
4. Lincoln's secretary was named Kennedy. Kennedy's secretary was named Lincoln.
5. Both men were shot in the presence of their wives and died on a Friday.
6. Each wife had lost a child while living at the White House.
7. Both men were killed by a bullet that entered the head from behind.
8. Lincoln was shot in Ford's Theater. Kennedy was shot in a Lincoln convertible made by the Ford Motor Company.
9. Both men were succeeded by vice-presidents named Johnson, who were southern Democrats and former senators.
10. Lincoln's successor was Andrew Johnson, who was born in 1808. Kennedy's successor was Lyndon Johnson, who was born in 1908.
11. Both assassins were Southern sympathizers who held extremist views.
12. Both assassins were killed before they could be brought to trial.
13. Booth shot Lincoln in a theater and fled to a warehouse. Oswald shot Kennedy from a warehouse and fled to a theater.
14. Their names, Lincoln and Kennedy, each have seven letters.
15. Andrew Johnson and Lyndon Johnson each have thirteen letters.

16. John Wilkes Booth and Lee Harvey Oswald each have fifteen letters.
17. Lincoln's secretary, Miss Kennedy, told him not to go to the theater. Kennedy's secretary, Miss Lincoln, told him not to go to Dallas.

When a normal, rational person reads one or two stories of this nature, he or she will understandably attribute it to coincidence. After all, *someone* has to win the lottery, right? But as I started looking into the matter, I saw that the sheer number of such accounts—even the verified ones—is simply startling. How do you explain all the Lincoln/Kennedy connections? Or how do you explain this documented example of synchronicity, made famous by Dr. Carl Jung:

> *French writer Émile Deschamps was treated to some plum pudding by a stranger named Monsieur de Fortgibu in 1805. He didn't try plum pudding again for ten years. Then, in 1815, he saw plum pudding on the menu of a Paris restaurant and tried to order some, but the waiter told him the last dish had already been served to another customer. Who was this customer? Monsieur de Fortgibu. Seventeen years later, in 1832, Émile Deschamps was at a diner, and was once again offered plum pudding. Remembering the earlier incident, he casually remarked to friends that the only thing missing was de Fortgibu, who then entered the room.*[2]

Jung coined the word "synchronicity" to describe what he called "temporally coincident occurrences of a-causal events," or, in other words, a pattern of connection that cannot be explained by conventional cause-and-effect explanations.

The Physical and the Meta-Physical

Over time, I became more comfortable with the idea that there is more to life than the physical. Of course, we live in a physical world. Drop

---

[2] Jung, C. G., *Synchronicity: An Acausal Connecting Principle*, from *The Collected Works of C. G. Jung*, vol. 8, page 15, Princeton/Bollingen, 1973.

a ball and it falls to the ground because of gravity. Use your muscles and apply counter-force and it will go up in the air, for a while. Hit me and I will hurt. These are manifestations of the physical world. Ignore physical realities at your own peril.

But there is also more than the physical world. There is the metaphysical. The supernatural. There are things that go on beyond our normal understanding. Physical realities, outer knowledge, simply cannot explain the examples mentioned here and the many thousands that weren't mentioned. Rationality is crucial to life, but many of us recognize that there is something beyond rationality as well. Since few of us experience a large number of instances of obvious synchronicity in a short period of time, we tend to ignore the phenomenon and move on. It is an understandable reaction.

But we shouldn't ignore this important element of life. Sensing the supernatural is a universal phenomenon. It encourages us to look for explanations. To appreciate that maybe, just maybe, there are things going on beyond human understanding. There are forces at work that we cannot fully understand. Sensing the supernatural opens the mind—and heart—to the world of the spirit. To bringing spirituality into one's life. To sensing God.

It's the Food
Memories of chicken soup and matzah balls

I'm Jewish because of the food.
No, really. What, other people get to eat cardboard every day for an entire week every spring? Or how about Manishewitz wine—would anyone who *isn't* Jewish ever choose to drink it once, let alone every year? My personal favorite is being served hot chicken soup with *matzah* balls even though it is August and 110 degrees in the shade. We are indeed a fortunate People.

The whole Jewish food thing reminds me of Woody Allen's description of two cranky women in a restaurant. One says, "The food here is terrible!"

"Yes," the other adds, "and such small portions!"

Once—only once—I had the audacity to leave something on my plate while eating at my grandmother's house during the holidays. The poor woman looked at me as if her best friend died, her favorite soap opera star was in a traffic accident, and the toilet backed up—all at the same time. I quickly finished the food, at which point she promptly filled up my plate again. There is no way out. If you eat, you eat again. And it you don't eat, you feel so guilty that you eat even more.

I do have some good Jewish food memories. On Passover there is a food called *charoset*. It is made of apples, nuts, and wine, and is supposed to represent the mortar the Jews used to make the pyramids in Egypt when we were slaves. I like the stuff. Most families make a small amount for the seder plate and everyone uses a little bit on *matzah*. Not my *Bubbe*. She put in three times the wine called for in the recipe. No wonder we enjoyed the seders so much—we were buzzed the entire time!

Other fond food memories include the aforementioned chicken soup with *matzah* balls on a *cold* day. There is nothing like it. Except maybe gefilte fish with some red beet horseradish. You haven't lived until you've tried Hungarian style.

Of course, I must admit that many other cultures have better food than we do. Chinese food. French food. What is Jewish food, anyway? Did King David eat borscht or brisket and kasha? There are many different styles of Jewish food from all over the world. So what is the big deal about Jewish food?

The real reason I love Jewish food is because food means family. A close family that comes together to eat. Where the kids actually want to be with their parents and the parents actually want to be with their kids. We catch up on our lives, joke around, and share the occasional story. I especially like the Passover Seder, with three generations and lots of cousins sitting around the table together. Great bonding.

The Jewish emphasis on family is one of the main reasons that I love being Jewish.

Staying strong Jewishly is the best way I know of keeping a family strong and of ensuring that my children will also want to create loving (and laughing!) families. Jewish holidays are family centered. Every Friday night we have plenty of time together. That connection builds the bonds that encourage us to connect the rest of the week as well. And then there are the holidays, coming often, with all the wonderful memories they leave. And let us not forget the life-cycle events. Family circumcisions and baby namings, weddings, and Bar and Bat Mitzvahs.

All this stuff means a lot to me. For instance, I cried at my son's Bar Mitzvah. When they handed me the bill.

But really, after I recovered, I cried again. I really wasn't prepared for how I would feel.

I remember looking around and saying to myself, "Who are these people and why am I paying for their meals?"

In truth, it was a very emotional time. I was thinking to myself, "This is it. This is what it is all about." My son gave a great speech. My wife was amazing, organized the whole thing in a classy but not crassy way. Our whole family came together, surrounded by cousins, aunts and uncles and of course many friends and other relatives.

Perhaps I'm wrong, but the communities in which I see the best attitudes towards family life are immigrant communities and religious communities. I'm not Mexican, Chinese, or anything else exotic. I'm not a Mormon.

I'm proudly Jewish—and I love the Jewish emphasis on family. With or without the *matzah* balls.

Mendel Rosenbaum
Finding God in Block B

No one knew where or how he got it. Did he hide it somewhere in his clothing? Did he bribe a guard? Did he retrieve it from a dead body? Feivel Zlotnik never revealed the secret of how he came to be the possessor of the only prayer book in Auschwitz's Block B. It was a small, thin, leather bound volume. The gilded edges of the pages had lost their color and the name that had once been embossed on the cover was by now indecipherable. But aside from these external signs of use, and a few frayed pages scattered throughout, the prayer book had fared remarkably well despite the heavy use that its tear-soaked pages revealed.

And heavily used it was. Thousands of men were housed in the block, with "new recruits" replacing old victims as soon as the latter were killed by harsh slave labor, starvation, or Zyklon B. Many of those who had grown up observant knew the daily prayers by heart. Yet they lined up to hold it, even for a moment. Caressing the prayer book was akin to holding their mother's hand or visiting their hometown. It reminded them of a different world. And there were others in line who had never or rarely prayed before Auschwitz.

Dr. Rosenbaum from Hamburg was one of them. He was a man of culture and sophistication. He read Goethe. He listened to Wagner. He fought proudly for Germany in the First World War. Refusing to leave his beloved Deutschland when he had the chance, he dismissed Hitler's rise as an aberration, a "temporary mistake" on the part of a great people. The murder of his dear wife and beloved child represented cognitive dissonance: his mind could not believe what his eyes and ears had witnessed. By the time he arrived in Auschwitz, he was a broken man. His identity was intimately tied with Germany, and Germany had turned its back on him to reveal its ugliness. But he wasn't completely broken as he watched with fascination other exhausted Jewish prisoners praying in the back of the barracks. He marveled at the reverence and love with which the camp inmates treated the prayer book.

"Who do you pray to, Zlotnik?" he asked. "Is God in this place? Is God anywhere? Do you really still believe in Him?"

"And who do you believe in, Professor? In man?" Zlotnik responded. They had long discussions about God, religion, the nature of evil and the seeming disappearance of good. For the first time in his forty-seven years, Dr. Rosenbaum felt connected to the Eastern European Jews that he had once disparaged. But he still didn't try to hold the prayer book. One night, unbeknown to anyone, he silently slipped out of bed and removed the prayer book from its hiding place. He held it closely. And he began to cry. He cried for his wife and child. He cried for the smoke rising from the ovens close by. He cried for his People. And he cried at the realization that it took tragedy to make him feel like a Jew.

Chain of Tradition[1]
Who did you receive the tradition from?

In daily life throughout the ages, the transmission of Judaism has occurred through mothers and fathers teaching their children.

Jewish scholars have had a special responsibility for safeguarding and transmitting our heritage and identity.

Thankfully, this chain of transmission itself has been carefully preserved. We know how the tradition was passed down, generation to generation:

> Moses received the tradition[2] from God.[3]
>
> Joshua received the tradition from Moses.

---

1. The "Chain of Transmission" of Torah has been carefully documented throughout our 3300 year history. In truth, there are numerous chains of transmissions with many overlapping teachers, students, and parents. Maimonides listed many of the generations in his introduction to the *Mishnah Torah*. Rabbi L. Kelemen did extensive research in this area (including careful verification of sources). Books on the subject include *Challenge of Sinai* and *Legacy of Sinai*, both by Zechariah Fendel (Hashkafa Publications, N.Y.).
2. Can the first transmission of Judaism truly be categorized as a "tradition?" I'll leave it to the experts to figure it out. For our purposes here, I use the word tradition to mean the body of knowledge, customs, identity, allegiance, and feelings we know as Judaism. Others may refer to this as Jewish identity, or Torah.
3. At Mount Sinai, in 1312 BCE.

Pinchas received the tradition from Joshua.
Eli received the tradition from Pinchas.
Samuel received the tradition from Eli.
David received the tradition from Samuel.
Achiah received the tradition from David.
Elijah received the tradition from Achiah.
Elisha received the tradition from Elijah.
Yehoyada received the tradition from Elisha.
Zechariah received the tradition from Yehoyada.
Hoshea received the tradition from Zechariah.
Amos received the tradition from Hoshea.
Isaiah received the tradition from Amos.
Michah received the tradition from Isaiah.
Yoel received the tradition from Michah.
Nachum received the tradition from Yoel.
Chabakuk received the tradition from Nachum.
Tzefaniah received the tradition from Chabakuk.
Jeremiah received the tradition from Tzefaniah.
Baruch received the tradition from Jeremiah.
Ezra received the tradition from Baruch.
Shimon Hatzaddik received the tradition from Ezra.
Antigonus of Socho received the tradition from Shimon Hatzaddik.
Yosi ben Yo'ezer and Yosef ben Yochanan received the tradition from Antigonus of Socho.
Yehoshua ben Prachya and Nitai of Arbel received the tradition from Yosi ben Yo'ezer and Yosef ben Yochanan.
Yehuda ben Tabai and Shimon ben Shetach received the tradition from Yehoshua ben Prachya and Nitai of Arbel.

*Shmaya and Avtalyon received the tradition
from Yehuda ben Tabai and Shimon ben Shetach.*

*Hillel and Shammai received the tradition
from Shmaya and Avtalyon.*

*Rabban Shimon ben Hillel received the tradition
from Hillel and Shammai.*

*Rabban Gamliel Hazaken received the tradition
from Rabban Shimon ben Hillel.*[4]

*Rav Shimon ben Gamliel received the tradition
from Rabban Gamliel Hazaken.*

*Rabban Gamliel received the tradition
from Rav Shimon ben Gamliel.*

Rabban Shimon received the tradition from Rabban Gamliel.

*Rabbi Yehuda Hanasi received the tradition
from Rabban Shimon.*

*Rav, Shmuel, and Rabbi Yochanan received the tradition
from Rabbi Yehuda Hanasi.*[5]

*Rav Huna received the tradition from Rav, Shmuel,
and Rabbi Yochanan.*

Rabbah received the tradition from Rav Huna.

Rava received the tradition from Rabbah.

Rav Ashi received the tradition from Rava.[6]

Rafram received the tradition from Rav Ashi.

Rav Sama B'rei d'Rava received the tradition from Rafram.

Rav Yosi received the tradition from Rav Sama B'rei d'Rava.

Rav Simonia received the tradition from Rav Yosi.

---

4   In some versions, he received the tradition from Yonasan son of Uziel, who in turn received it from Shimon son of Hillel.
5   In some versions, there was one generation, or part of one, in between this and the previous generation, which included Rabban Gamliel III, Bar Kappara, and others.
6   In some versions, he followed Rav Papa and Rav Huna B'rei de Rav Yehoshua, who studied under Abaye and Rava.

Rav Ravoi Me-Rov received the tradition from Rav Simonia.

Mar Chanan Me-Ashkaya received the tradition from Rav Ravoi Me-Rov.

Rav Mari received the tradition from Mar Chanan Me-Ashkaya.

Rav Chana Gaon[7] received the tradition from Rav Mari.

Mar Rav Rava received the tradition from Rav Chana Gaon.

Rav Busai received the tradition from Mar Rav Rava.

Mar Rav Huna Mari received the tradition from Rav Busai.

Mar Rav Chiyah Me-Mishan received the tradition from Mar Rav Huna Mari.

Mar Ravyah received the tradition from Mar Rav Chiyah Me-Mishan.

Mar Rav Natronai received the tradition from Mar Ravyah.

Mar Rav Yebuda received the tradition from Mar Rav Natronai.

Mar Rav Yosef received the tradition from Mar Rav Yebuda.

Mar Rav Shmuel received the tradition from Mar Rav Yosef.

Mar Rav Natroi Kahana received the tradition from Mar Rav Shmuel.

Mar Rav Avraham Kahana received the tradition from Mar Rav Natroi Kahana.

Mar Rav Dodai received the tradition from Mar Rav Avraham Kahana.

Rav Chananya received the tradition from Mar Rav Dodai.

Rav Malka received the tradition from Rav Chananya.

Mar Rav Rava received the tradition from Rav Malka.

Mar Rav Shinoi received the tradition from Mar Rav Rava.

---

[7] Two different chains of transmission begin here, following either the Pumbedisa or Sura academies' leaders.

Mar Rav Chaninah Gaon Kahana received the tradition from Mar Rav Shinoi.

Mar Rav Huna Mar Halevi received the tradition from Mar Rav Chaninah Gaon Kahana.

Mar Rav Menasheh received the tradition from Mar Rav Huna Mar Halevi.

Mar Rav Yeshaya Halevi received the tradition from Mar Rav Menasheh.

Mar Rav Kahanah Gaon received the tradition from Mar Rav Yeshaya Halevi.

Mar Rav Yosef received the tradition from Mar Rav Kahanah Gaon.

Mar Rav Ibomai Gaon received the tradition from Mar Rav Yosef.

Mar Rav Yosef received the tradition from Mar Rav Ibomai Gaon.

Mar Rav Avraham received the tradition from Mar Rav Yosef.

Mar Rav Yosef received the tradition from Mar Rav Avraham.

Mar Rav Yitzchak received the tradition from Mar Rav Yosef.

Mar Rav Yosef received the tradition from Mar Rav Yitzchak.

Mar Rav Poltoi received the tradition from Mar Rav Yosef.

Mar Rav Achai Kahana received the tradition from Mar Rav Poltoi.

Mar Rav Menachem received the tradition from Mar Rav Achai Kahana.

Mar Rav Matisyahu received the tradition from Mar Rav Menachem.

Rav Mar Abba received the tradition from Mar Rav Matisyahu.

Mar Rav Tzemach Gaon received the tradition from Rav Mar Abba.

Mar Rav Hai Gaon received the tradition
from Mar Rav Tzemach Gaon.

Mar Rav Kimoi Gaon received the tradition
from Mar Rav Hai Gaon.

Mar Rav Yehuda received the tradition
from Mar Rav Kimoi Gaon.

Mar Rav Mevasser Kahana Gaon received the tradition
from Mar Rav Yehuda.

Rav Kohen Tzedek received the tradition
from Mar Rav Mevasser Kahana Gaon.

Mar Rav Tzemach Gaon received the tradition
from Rav Kohen Tzedek.

Rav Chaninah Gaon received the tradition
from Mar Rav Tzemach Gaon.

Mar Rav Aharon Hakohen received the tradition
from Rav Chaninah Gaon.

Mar Rav Nechemiah received the tradition
from Mar Rav Aharon Hakohen.

Rav Sherirah Gaon received the tradition
from Mar Rav Nechemiah.

Meshulam Hagadol received the tradition
from Rav Sherirah Gaon.

Rav Gershom Me'or Hagolah received the tradition
from Meshulam Hagadol.

Rav Yaakov ben Yakar received the tradition
from Rav Gershom Me'or Hagolah.

Rav Shlomo Yitzchaki (Rashi) received the tradition
from Rav Yaakov ben Yakar.

R' Shmuel ben Meir (Rashbam) received the tradition
from Rav Shlomo Yitzchaki.

R' Yaakov ben Meir (Rabbenu Tam) received the tradition
from R' Shmuel ben Meir.

Eliezer Me-Metz received the tradition from R' Yaakov ben Meir.

Rokeach received the tradition from Eliezer Me-Metz.

R' Yitzchak of Vienna (Ohr Zaruah) received the tradition from Rokeach.

Rav Meir of Rothenberg received the tradition from R' Yitzchak of Vienna.

R' Yitzchak of Duren (Sha'arei Durah) received the tradition from Rav Meir of Rothenberg.

R' Alexander Zuslin Hakohen (Agudah) received the tradition from R' Yitzchak of Duren.

Meir bar Baruch Halevi received the tradition from R' Alexander Zuslin Hakohen.

R' Shalom of Neustadt received the tradition from Meir bar Baruch Halevi.

R' Yaakov Moelin (Maharil) received the tradition from R' Shalom of Neustadt.

R' Yisrael Isserlein (Trumas Hadeshen) received the tradition from R' Yaakov Moelin.

R' Tavoli received the tradition from R' Yisrael Isserlein.

Rabbi Yaakov Margolies received the tradition from R' Tavoli.

Rabbi Yaakov Pollak received the tradition from Rabbi Yaakov Margolies.

Rabbi Shalom Shachna received the tradition from Rabbi Yaakov Pollak.

Rabbi Moshe Isserles (Rama) received the tradition from Rabbi Shalom Shachna.

Rabbi Yehoshua Falk Katz received the tradition from Rabbi Moshe Isserles.

Rabbi Naftali Hirsch ben Pesachya received the tradition from Rabbi Yehoshua Falk Katz .

Rabbi Moshe Rivkas (Be'er Hagolah) received the tradition from Rabbi Naftali Hirsch ben Pesachya.

Rabbi Avraham Gombiner received the tradition from Rabbi Moshe Rivkas.

Rabbi Moshe Kramer received the tradition from Rabbi Avraham Gombiner.

Rabbi Eliyahu Chasid received the tradition from Rabbi Moshe Kramer.

Rabbi Yissachar Ber received the tradition from Rabbi Eliyahu Chasid.

Rabbi Shlomo Zalman received the tradition from Rabbi Yissachar Ber.

Rabbi Eliyahu Kramer (Vilna Gaon) received the tradition from Rabbi Shlomo Zalman.

Rabbi Chaim Volozhiner received the tradition from Rabbi Eliyahu Kramer.

Rabbi Yosef Zundel of Salant received the tradition from Rabbi Chaim Volozhiner.

Rabbi Yisrael Salanter received the tradition from Rabbi Yosef Zundel of Salant.

Rabbi Simcha Zissel Ziv (Alter of Kelm) received the tradition from Rabbi Yisrael Salanter.

Rabbi Nosson Zvi Finkel (Alter of Slobodka) received the tradition from Rabbi Simcha Zissel Ziv.

My great-grandfather received the tradition from Rabbi Nosson Zvi Finkel.

My grandfather received the tradition from my great-grandfather.

My father received the tradition from my grandfather.

I received the tradition from my father.

My children will receive it from me.

Who did you receive the tradition from?

Who will you pass it on to?

The Dalai Lama
Surprising advice from the East

When my three-year stint in the Israel Defense Forces (IDF) was over, I did what many Israelis do: travel to the East. India. Nepal. Thailand. There are tens of thousands of young Israelis in these countries at any given time. We grow up in a small country surrounded by enemies. Once our military service is complete, we need a break. We want to breathe. To relax. There are, in fact, so many Israelis that one finds signs in Hebrew in more than a few backpacker spots.

I deserved and needed a break. So I worked for a while to make some money, convinced my parents to lend me some more, and flew to India. In truth, at the time, my goals were simple: (a) relax on a beach; (b) relax on a beach; and (c) relax on a beach. When the money started to run out, I waited tables part-time at an Israeli-owned bar. Life was good and I enjoyed it this way for almost two years.

Throughout this time in India, I would observe the locals as well as the foreigners coming to the East to get "enlightened." I grew up in the northern part of Tel Aviv. We had no religion at all. My family was not anti-religion per se, though some of my friends certainly were. We simply had no interest. Life was about life. Living well. Having fun. Giving back something. While there are many religious Jews in the army, there weren't any in my unit. So witnessing the Indian devotion to their temples and gods, and meeting people—good, normal people—who talked about meditation, karma, and enlightenment was fascinating for me. I didn't do anything about it for a long time, but somewhere in the back of my mind, I knew that before leaving India I should check it all out.

The catalyst was Maria. Maria was a twenty-three-year-old Italian student who came to the restaurant. She was jet-lagged and I was working late so we got to talking. She was intelligent, well educated, and going to an Ashram for six weeks. I expressed surprise. She looked at me simply and said, "Look into your heart. What do you really think life is about? Drinking and smoking and partying? A nice car and a nice house? Is that what you *really* believe we are here for? Inside, you know there is more. The East will teach you what else there is." With that, Maria left the restaurant.

Two weeks later, so did I. For good. I went north to Dharamsala, spiritual center of Tibetan Buddhism and home of the famed Dalai Lama.

It was winter. Northern India was cold. And the Ashram was spartan. The food was simple. People spoke quietly and sat still. I wasn't prepared for the change and it was hard. But I was at a stage in life where I really didn't know what to do or what life was about. I lacked direction. I don't mean to say I was lost or lonely or unhappy. I wasn't. Simply that I was unclear as to what my goal in life was. So the Ashram was a great refuge from all the dance music, noise, busyness, and distractions that I had been used to. It gave me a chance to think. Even on the beach in India, I hadn't really had quiet like I found in the Ashram. And, once I got used to it, I loved it. I cherished the silence. I studied myself in a deeper way than I ever had in school. I *thought* deeper.

I considered what most of my friends and acquaintances were doing. Sitting on a beach. Backpacking through South America. And I thought to myself, why? So they travel and see the world and learn about different cultures. What next? Or they enter the rat race to make money. To do what with?

I knew there was more. I sensed it. So, for the first time in my life, I got in touch with spirituality. I meditated. I sensed something beyond myself. I came to believe in Karma. My initial two months in the Ashram stretched and stretched longer and longer. Two and a half years later, I was an advanced student of Tibetan Buddhism. My head was shaved and I resembled a Tibetan Monk. And I aspired to be one. To my family's dismay, I had no intention of leaving Dharamsala. I had found an inner peace that no one I knew from Tel Aviv had ever imagined.

Meeting the Dalai Lama

I had heard the Dalai Lama speak on many occasions and had seen him walking almost daily. It was possible to obtain a short (e.g. 5 minute) audience with him, although the waiting list was very long. For the first couple of years I had nothing to say and nothing to ask, so I didn't request a meeting. But I had some specific theological questions that mid-level monks had not been able to answer fully, so I requested a private audience. About two months later, my turn came.

I entered his chamber. I bowed in respect. I sat down before him. In Buddhist custom, a lower-level initiate does not speak first to a higher-level monk. So of course, I maintained a respectful silence and waited for the Dalai Lama to greet me or give me permission to speak. He looked at me, whispered something briefly to his advisors, who nodded back. He put his hands forward in greeting and granted me permission to speak. I asked my first question. He didn't answer. Rather, he looked at me, cocked his head a little bit to the side, and said, "Where are you from?"

I was caught off guard. "Israel," I replied.

"And you are a Jew?" I was caught even more off guard. "Well, yes...I mean my parents are Jews...but..."

The Dalai Lama looked at me as a father looks at a son. "Why are you studying here? Judaism is the Mother Religion. You should go back to Israel and look into your own heritage. You have a tradition. Everything you seek is there."

As I try now to describe how I felt, only one word comes to mind: angry. Very, very angry. What had being Jewish ever given me? I had grown up in a small country that was always being attacked. No one I knew had any real understanding of what life was about. Peoples' lives were filled with movies, television, and sports. Finally, I had found something real. I meditated. I felt at peace. I touched enlightenment. And here, I was being told to go home. How dare he? I was furious.

Though I tried, I couldn't really meditate anymore. Too many negative thoughts and self-doubts. How could I continue with Buddhism or any Eastern path? After all, the single most respected figure in the Eastern world, the Dalai Lama, had told me to stop being a Buddhist and go home.

I struggled with this major life change and within a few weeks I realized that I couldn't stay in India. And, lacking money and other options, I called home and asked my parents to pay for a ticket back to Israel, which they gladly did.

Re-adjusting to Tel Aviv was not easy. I hadn't seen my family or friends for over four years. I was trying to recover from the rejection I felt in India. I wasn't comfortable meditating or being involved in Eastern religions. And yet, I was not interested in the superficial life of many of my compatriots.

After a couple of months of hiding out in my parents' house doing a lot of nothing, it was time to do something. So I got a job doing something I was good at. Waiting tables. It was poorly paid but the tips were good and I was living at home, so I was even able to put some money away.

As it turns out, the restaurant was kosher. No shellfish. No mixing of milk and meat. After experiencing Buddhist diet restrictions, I was no longer disdainful of the effect of diet on a person's whole being. The other waiter was religious, a soldier who had just been released from the army. The Dalai Lama's words kept ringing in my ears. He had told me to look into my own heritage and my own religion. So I started asking the waiter questions. And the *mashgiach*, the "kosher supervisor" who came in twice a week to make sure the restaurant was following the rules. While most of our clients were not observant Jews, some were—and I asked them as well. I read some books. I went to some lectures. I joined the kosher supervisor for a traditional Shabbat at his home (my first one, at the age of twenty-five).

I'm not what is commonly called a "religious Jew." I'm moving slowly. I don't wear a *kippah*. I don't follow all the rules. But I have come home. I'm open and hoping to grow. I see in Judaism an amazing tradition of spirituality. I now understand Judaism's wisdom in taking practical life (eating, working, etc) and *spiritualizing* it through prayer, blessings, and contemplation. Perhaps most importantly, I have become proud, extremely proud, to be the bearer of a tradition that has brought spirituality into the world. To belong to the "Mother Religion." I have become a proud, connected Jew. And I owe it to the Dalai Lama.

May God Bless You, Eric Jones
Crossing my red lines

Eric and I were very different. He played football. I played chess. He was class president. I was part of the computer club. He was tall and blond. I wasn't. You get the picture.

We met in summer camp when we were twelve years old. We were roommates and spent hours talking to each other. Eric transferred to my school that year, and his family moved to within biking distance of my house. Despite our differences, we somehow became very close friends. I would even say that he was my best friend during high school, and I think I was his.

His family had a cottage on a lake in the mountains. Every summer I'd go up for a few days and swim and canoe with him. For a lower-middle class city boy like me, the air and water and fun were heaven. Some of my best memories are from those summer visits. Every winter break, his family would go up to the cottage and spend a couple of weeks skiing and sledding. I would stay home and do...nothing much.

One year, in tenth grade, he invited me to come up for the whole winter vacation. His brother wasn't coming home that winter so there was room and his parents were happy for him to have a friend. He knew I wouldn't be doing much of anything during the break. And he knew my parents would be happy that I turn off the television and get some fresh air and exercise. How could I say no? Why should I say no? I couldn't wait.

The first three days were action-packed. We went skating on the frozen lake. We went sledding down the local hills. We went skiing. We talked at night and drank hot cocoa.

The next day his family went "looking for a tree." Of course, I went along—I was so happy to be included in their family vacation that I happily said yes to anything and everything.

Believe it not, at first it didn't register what they meant by looking for a tree. Only when we pulled into this huge lot filled with evergreens did I realize what tree they were looking for. Maybe it was the huge sign reading, "Christmas Trees Here" that gave it away. No harm in helping them choose a tree, is there? After all, I was a guest. So I just kind of smiled, threw snowballs back and forth with Eric and his sisters, and watched the proceedings.

Next, they loaded the tree on their car, tied it to the roof, and drove home. The afternoon was spent decorating the tree. Carrying in boxes of tinsel and other decorations from the storage room, making cutouts, attaching the balls. Hanging stockings. There were no other activities that afternoon and everyone was sitting around enjoying. I didn't want to offend anyone by refusing to participate. Eric had been at my house for many Jewish holidays over the years and always been very respectful and interested. So I helped decorate the tree.

Late that afternoon was "Christmas Dinner." I'd heard the phrase before but I had no idea what it meant. In Eric's family, and in many others, it was the main event of the day. Everyone gets together, including cousins, grandparents, and aunts and uncles for a feast. There was a lot of food (and drink, for the adults) on the table. Place settings were in red and green. The table was covered with various breads, salads, and side dishes.

One plate had sausages wrapped in bacon. In my family, pig was like poison. It was something that Jews simply *did not* eat. Ever.

Don't do this to me, God. Don't make this a scene.

But I caught myself. There is plenty of other food on the table. I can do this. No one needs to know.

Then Eric's sister announced that the main dishes were being brought in. Everyone applauded. Eric's father walked in with a large silver serving platter. On it was what looked like an entire pig with an apple in its mouth.

The pig was staring right at me. And smirking.

I think I even heard it laugh.

I'm in trouble, I thought to myself. Then Eric's mother yelled from the kitchen, "Wait. It's not over. Here comes the Turkey."

I looked up at Heaven and smiled,

Thank You. Thank You.

I'll never take the air out of the principal's tires again, ever.

I promise. Thank You.

Then I saw the platter than Eric's mother was carrying. There were dozens of slices of bacon dripping over the turkey. We're talking about a LOT of oozing bacon stuff.

Thanks for nothing....

I felt like throwing up.

Hey, that's not a bad idea, I thought quickly. Maybe I'll just throw up and be excused from the meal. Nah. Too obvious. Besides, I could never put my fingers down my throat. If it works, the barf gets all over your hands. Gross.

Maybe I'll just fill my plate with other foods and no one will notice? That isn't likely to work—everyone is passing their plates for a serving of one of the main dishes. Maybe I'll just politely tell them I'm not so hungry? No way—this is the first real meal since breakfast. They know I'm hungry.

Maybe I can explain? Suddenly I remembered a scene from a Charles Dickens novel. The little boy is living in a dirty, uncaring orphanage. They get very little food. He is hungry. So he approaches the adult at the front of the room with his empty little bowl and says, "Please sir, I want some more." Two hundred silent little heads turn in shock. You could hear a pin drop. The cruel headmaster responds with fury. If I refuse the food, they'll know. It'll be a scene. I'll be Oliver Twist. Oliver Twist-berg.

What will they know? That I'm Jewish? They already know I'm Jewish. My name is David Friedberg.

If I refuse the food, they'll know I'm different.

But they know I'm different. They have blond hair, blue eyes, and small noses. I'm like Neanderthal Man.

Here is the real problem: If I don't eat, they'll think that I think that I'm better than they are. It'll make them very uncomfortable. There will be silence and shock. "You mean our food is not good enough for you?"

I don't think I'm better. Heck, I spend most of my waking hours dreaming I was Eric. I'm just different and there are certain red lines I won't cross. Like making the cross. Or eating pig. Or playing in the World Series on Yom Kippur...

No. I was not going to eat the pig. But how could I get out of this mess without insulting their whole family, who had been so good to me?

Suddenly, Eric, who was sitting beside me, announced, "Dad, you don't have to serve us. Davie and I were starving so we ate before. See the piece missing from the Turkey? It was delicious. Can we just sit here with you and have dessert?"

May God bless you, Eric Jones. May He bless you with health, wealth, and a Super Bowl ring. May you merit to see your children and grandchildren healthy, wealthy, and happy. May you find a gorgeous wife who knows how to cook and laughs at your stupid jokes. May you merit a special place in the World to Come. Right beside Elvis. You are the best friend a person ever had. Better than a brother (certainly my brother). I owe you my life. I am your servant. I'll throw myself in a puddle and let you walk across my back to stay dry. Happily...I'll...

"What?" Mr. Jones was not happy. "Your mother spent three days cooking and you couldn't wait like the rest of us? What kind of behavior is that? I can't believe this. If there is one meal a year..."

Mrs. Jones stared at the bacon-turkey with the supposed "missing piece." Then she looked at Eric. And at me. She then winked at us and said to her husband, "Don't get upset, Paul. It is Christmas, after all. I told the boys it was okay. They're growing boys and I didn't want them hungry and grouchy all day. But don't you boys think you're getting dessert right away. You fill up those plates with salads if you want dessert."

May God bless you, Mrs. Jones. May He bless you with health, wealth, and a new diamond ring. May you merit to see your children and grandchildren healthy, wealthy, and happy. May your husband take out the garbage, put his socks in the hamper, and laugh at your jokes. May you merit a special place in the World to Come, beside Barry Manilow. You are the best mother a person could ever have (aside from my mother, of course. Like a stepmother. But not a wicked one.) I owe you my life. I am your servant. I'll throw myself in a puddle and let you walk across my back to stay dry. Happily...I'll...

The meal went on uneventfully. They talked about football, past Christmas meals, and a lot of other things that I didn't really focus on. I was still recovering from The Pig Challenge.

When the meal was over, everybody went for a walk outside. Eric and I walked ahead.

"Eric. I don't know what to say. Thank you. I'm sorry. I didn't mean to ruin your meal. I feel terrible. You didn't even get to eat. And your mom spent all that time cooking."

"Don't be sorry. I brought you here and should've thought about what would happen. I'm sorry that I put you in such a bad position. I've been at your house for many holidays and you've always made me comfortable and then I put you in-between a rock and a...pig. I ate plenty. And don't worry about my mom. In the kitchen she whispered to me that she felt bad she hadn't made something you'd be comfortable eating. She was proud of you for sticking to your religion. So am I."

United Nations
The Jewish vision for the world

The world is filled with many beautiful nations. Each has a role. Some gave the world great food. Some wine. Some music. The Greeks came up with democracy. I don't downplay the contributions of these or other peoples. And I don't underestimate ours.

The ancient world (Egypt, Assyria, Greece, Rome, etc.) was based on might. The most admired were the strongest and toughest. Killing for sport was common. Killing in war was glorious. The ancients actually had gods of war. The most famous was Mars, one of the most respected of all the gods in Roman society. Romans prided themselves in being descendants of Mars. War was so extolled that its god, Mars, had his own day of the week: Tuesday was called *Martis Dies* (still today *Martes* in Spanish, and *Mardi* in French).

The world has come a long way from its glorification of war. While far from perfect, the United Nations represents the dream of universal peace. A large memorial plaque outside the UN reads:

> They shall beat their swords into ploughshares, and their spears into pruning hooks; nation shall not lift up sword against nation, neither shall they learn war anymore.

These famous words represent the central ideal of the United Nations itself—to end war and usher in an age of peace and brotherhood.

Where do these words come from? Where does this vision of peace and brotherhood come from? Not from the Greeks, Romans, Egyptians, Assyrians or other ancient peoples. They venerated war. The words that represent the vision of peace come from the Jewish prophet, Isaiah, chapter 2, verse 4.

When the world looks to a vision of universal peace, it looks to the Jewish vision. In the ancient world, human life had no value. We taught that every human being was created in the Divine Image. In the ancient world, war was glorified. We gave the world its vision of peace. In the ancient world, people rarely felt any connection to others who were different than they were. We taught that there was one Father in Heaven and therefore we are all children of the same God; brothers, sisters and cousins.

While the world has progressed in its aspirations and actions, even today, much of the world idolizes money, power, lust, and greed. We focus on goodness, giving, humility, and Godliness.

This is why I am proud to be Jewish.

Why Stay Jewish
Why bother, anyway?

It was 1994. The Jewish community center in Buenos Aires, Argentina, had just been blown up by terrorists. Eighty-five people were killed and hundreds wounded. Because of the large loss of life, indications that radical Muslim terrorists were involved, and an otherwise slow news day, the attack was getting tremendous news coverage.

My co-workers were mostly Protestants with a couple of Catholics thrown in. I was the only Jew. Peter had always seemed very curious about Judaism. He went out of his way to wish me a Happy Chanukah, knew when Rosh Hashana was, and was in general very respectful of my Jewish background.

That morning, I caught him glancing at me a few times. There was clearly something he wanted to say, but he was hesitating. I decided to just ask him directly, "Pete—is everything okay? Something you want to talk about?"

"Well, yes, actually," he responded. "I'm not sure how to ask this, and please don't take any offense, but I don't understand. All the centuries of persecution, hatred, and now wars and terrorism. I mean, for someone who is a believing Jew, I guess they do what they believe in. And I respect that. But, please forgive me; you are not a believing Jew. Why do you and people like you try so hard to stay Jewish? You identify as a Jew, and yet that label seems to bring trouble generation after generation. Why sacrifice so much? Why have to deal with the anti-Semitism, the attacks and the hate? In your position, I'd just disappear into the mainstream and avoid so many problems…"

I was caught off guard and mumbled something about history and identity. But I didn't really answer his question.

The truth is that my relationship to Judaism is complex. There are certain Jewish things that are crucial to me. I very much wanted to get married by a rabbi with a *chupah*. I go to synagogue on the High Holidays and attend a Passover seder. I am a strong supporter of Israel. And I want to be buried as a Jew.

On the other hand, as Peter pointed out, I don't go to synagogue very often. I can't read Hebrew, and have never been to Israel. So why bother?

Understanding Love

Can a person really explain why they love their spouse? We can come up with lots of reasons (sweet, caring, funny, etc.) why he/she is special, but countless other people surely share those qualities as well. What makes our "special someone" special?

Love. Beauty. Hope. Certain things are beyond words. They just *are*.

An art critic once interviewed Picasso about his works. He pointed to a certain painting and asked Picasso, "What were you trying to say with this painting?"

Picasso looked at the man with horror. "*Saying?*" Picasso asked incredulously. "If I wanted to *say* something, I would've written a poem. I *painted* a painting!"

Words can describe feelings. When spoken by a master, they can even evoke feelings. But they can never fully express the feelings themselves. Sometimes, words can even get in the way of true feelings.

Consider one of my favorite Walt Whitman poems, *When I Heard the Learn'd Astronomer:*

> When I heard the learn'd astronomer;
> When the proofs, the figures, were ranged in columns before me;

> When I was shown the charts and diagrams to add, divide, and measure them;
> When I, sitting, heard the astronomer, where he lectured with much applause in the lecture room,
> How soon unaccountable I became tired and sick;
> Till rising and gliding out I wander'd off by myself,
> In the mystical moist night-air, and from time to time,
> Looked up in perfect silence at the stars.

Words are limiting. Even logic itself is limiting. Love is beyond logic.

I remember a sermon I heard many years ago that stuck with me. We are the People of the Book. Our tradition is based on thinking, learning, questioning, and even arguing. Yet the very first letter of the Hebrew alphabet, the *aleph*, is silent. Why is this so? Because the first thing that we need to understand about words is that they are limited. While important, even necessary, all the words and logic in the world can only get a person so far. There is something beyond words. There is feeling. There is inner clarity. There is love. There is loyalty. There is...

The truth is that I may never be able to explain why being Jewish is so important to me. While there are many logical reasons to be Jewish, the ultimate reason for my Jewish attachment is beyond words and beyond logic. I can't explain it. But it is.

How Many Jews Does It Take to Screw In a Light Bulb?
Lessons from Jewish humor

An elderly Jewish man in Miami calls his son in New York and says, "I hate to ruin your day, but I have to tell you that your mother and I are divorcing. Forty-five years of misery is enough."

"Pop, what are you talking about?" the son screams.

"We can't stand the sight of each other any longer," the old man says. "We're sick of each other, and I'm sick of talking about this, so you call your sister in Chicago and tell her," and he hangs up. Frantic, the son calls his sister, who explodes on the phone. "Like heck they're getting divorced," she shouts. "I'll take care of this." She calls her father immediately and screams, "You are NOT getting divorced! Don't do a single thing until I get there. I'm calling my brother back and we'll both be there tomorrow. Until then, don't do a thing, DO YOU HEAR ME?" and hangs up. The old man hangs up the phone, turns to his wife, and smiles."Okay," he says, "they're coming for the Passover seder and paying their own airfares."

Jerry Seinfeld. Jackie Mason. Billy Crystal. Woody Allen. Jack Benny. Milton Berle. Mel Brooks. George Burns. Rodney Dangerfield. Bud Abbott (of Abbott and Costello). Lenny Bruce. Roseanne Barr. Jerry Lewis. Al Franken. Richard Lewis. Howie Mandel. Rick Moranis. David Schwimmer. Gary Shandling. Ben Stiller. Peter Sellers. Howard Stern. Gilda Radner. Henny Youngman. Most of the Vaudeville comedians. Judy Gold. Joan Rivers. Jon Stewart. Adam Sandler. Larry David. David Brenner. Lewis Black. Sandra Bernhard. David Cross. Jack Benny. Sacha Baron Cohen. Robert Klein. Alan King. Dave Attell. Jeffrey Ross. Paul Reiser. Chelsea Handler. Don Rickles. Sarah Silverman...The list goes on. It is quite an impressive list, especially when you consider that Jews represent about 1.5 percent of the American population. Jews are funny people. Personally, I'm glad. Because I love Jewish humor. It is wise. It is chutzpadik. It is non-reverential. Above all, it is funny.

A young woman brings her new fiancé home to meet her parents. After dinner, the father invites the young man to sit on the porch and have a drink. "So what are your plans?" the father asks. "I am a Torah scholar," he replies.

"A Torah scholar. Hmmm," the father says. "Admirable, but what will you do to provide for my daughter?"

"I will study," the young man replies, "and God will provide for us."

"And how will you buy a house?" asks the father. "I will study," the young man replies, "and God will provide for us."

"And children?" asks the father. "How will you support children?"

"God will provide," replies the fiancé.

The conversation proceeds like this, and to each of the father's practical questions, the young idealist answers that God will provide.

Later, the mother asks, "So, what happened?" The father answers, "The bad news is that he has no job and no plans. The good news is that he thinks I'm God."

One of the things I love most about Jewish humor is that we aren't afraid to laugh at ourselves. It is a sign of health to recognize and poke fun at your weaknesses.

Hebrew University in Jerusalem decided to field a rowing (crew) team. Unfortunately, they lost race after race. They practiced for hours every day, but never managed to come in any better than dead last. The coach finally decided to send someone to Boston to spy on the Harvard team. So he goes and hides in the bulrushes until he figures it out. Finally returning to the coach, the spy announces, "I figured out their secret—they have eight guys rowing and only one guy shouting."

Jewish mothers and grandmothers have been on the receiving end of more than a few Jewish jokes.

Harry Goldberg is the first Jewish boy to be elected president. He is very proud and phones his mother in New York to invite her to the inauguration.

Harry: "Mom, I've just been elected president! I want you to come to the inauguration."

Mother: "Harry, dear, you know I hate trains. I can't come all the way down to Washington."

Harry: "Mom! The president's mother is not going to take the train. Air Force One will pick you up; it is a very short flight."

Mother: "Harry, I hate hotels. Too crowded."

Harry: "Mom!! You will stay in the White House, with plenty of room to yourself. Please come."

Mother: "Harry! I have nothing to wear."

Harry: "I'm sending someone to take you shopping. New outfit is on me. You must come, Mom."

Mother: "Okay, okay, I'll come."

At the inauguration, the president's mother is seated on the platform with the other VIP's. As Harry is about to be sworn in, his mother elbows the man beside her and says, "Hey, you see that boy Harry? His brother is a very successful doctor!"

Or consider this:

A young Jewish mother walks her son to the school bus corner on his first day of kindergarten. "Behave, my *bubaleh*," she says. "Take good care of yourself and think about your mother, *tataleh*!"

"And come right back home on the bus, *schein kindaleh*. Your Mommy loves you a lot, my *ketsaleh*!" At the end of the school day, the bus comes back and she runs to her son and hugs him. "So what did my *pupaleh* learn on his first day of school?" The boy answers, "I learned that my name is David."

A Catholic friend of mine once commented that he loved Jewish people. I asked why and he responded, "I think it is because Jews are funny."

A rabbi, priest, and an imam are at an interfaith meeting. They are asked, "When you die and are placed in a casket and being eulogized, what would you like them to say about you?" The priest says, "I would like to hear them say that I was a good Christian and served my community well." The imam says, "I would like to hear them say that I was a good Muslim and served my community well." The rabbi smiles and replies, "I would like to hear them say, 'Look, he's moving!'"

A Jewish grandmother is babysitting her grandson at the beach. He has his pail and shovel and is digging in the sand on the ocean's edge like any child. All of a sudden, a gigantic wave barrels in from the ocean, scoops up the child, his pail and shovel, and sweeps them out to sea. The horrified grandmother shrieks in horror and starts pleading with God: "Please, please, my grandson, save him! You're a merciful God, and he is only a child. I'll be a good Jew. I'll light candles. I'll do anything." Immediately, a gigantic wave comes in, and deposits the little boy safely with his pail and shovel exactly where he was before. The grandmother looks him over with great relief and then turns to God: "His hat! He was wearing a hat!!"

Jewish men don't get off easily either.

Sidney telephones Rabbi Levy. He says, "Rabbi, I know tonight is Kol Nidre night, but there is a huge game tonight on TV. I'm sorry, Rabbi, I can't come. I can't miss this game."

Rabbi Levy replies, "Sidney, that's what video recorders are for." Sidney is surprised. "You mean I can tape Kol Nidre?"

Amazingly, even in the midst of the saddest of Jewish times, the Holocaust, Jews were able to boost their morale and emotionally resist through humor—at the Nazis' expense of course:

As Hitler's armies faced increasing setbacks, he asked his astrologer, "Am I going to lose the war?"

"Yes," the astrologer said.

"Then, am I going to die?" Hitler asked.

"Yes."

"When am I going to die?"

"On a Jewish holiday."

"But on what holiday?"

"Any day you die will be a Jewish holiday."

Goebbels was touring German schools. At one, he asked the students to call out patriotic slogans. "Heil Hitler," shouted one child. "Very good," said Goebbels.

"Deutschland über alles," another called out. "Excellent. How about a stronger slogan?" A hand shot up, and Goebbels nodded. "Our People shall live forever," the little boy said. "Wonderful," exclaimed Goebbels. "What is your name, young man?"

"Israel Goldberg."

What a People. Generation after generation, not harming anybody, we become society's scapegoat. How do we respond? Do we get angry? Do we take revenge? No. We develop a tradition of humor without parallel. What a People!

Love, Jewish Style
Judaism's effect on my marriage

I loved my father, of course, but I didn't want to marry him. He was short. I wanted tall. He was dark. I wanted blond. His eyes were brown. I wanted blue. He had a paunch. I wanted physique. He didn't drink or smoke. I wanted someone who would party hard. He was careful and responsible. I wanted someone who would bungee-jump, surf, and kick-box. Both my parents were Jewish. While I never admitted this openly, I wanted someone who wasn't.

High school. College. Europe. The Far East. I went anywhere I wanted. Did anything I wanted. To pay for my travels, adventures, and social life, I held many jobs: waitress, bicycle messenger, receptionist, salesperson, physical trainer, graphic artist, nanny, and more. Life took its course. I was happy. I was busy. I wasn't lacking anything.

Then my friends started getting married. When I was twenty-five, all of my friends were single. Within a few years, there were only a couple of us singles left. Paula, one of the other holdouts, and I became very close.

One Saturday night she goes out with a guy named Zack. The next morning, at 8:30 am, she calls me up and says that she just met my future husband.

I'm groggy and angry at the wake-up call. I misunderstand and think she said that she just met *her* future husband. Faking happiness as best as I can early on a Sunday morning, I say, "Congratulations. I'm really happy for you. Can we talk about this later?"

She responds, "Not my husband. YOUR husband. He wasn't right for me at all. Nothing in common. He felt the same way. We spent most of the evening talking about you. He's perfect for you and he's interested. He is picking you up for brunch at 11 a.m. He is really, really sweet. Very cute. Good job. If you make someone else your maid of honor, I'll kill you."

Now I was fully awake: "What?! You did what?! You gave a guy that you just met my name and address? And he is coming here? Today? Are you crazy? He could be an axe-murderer. Paula I can't believe..."

Paula was a no-nonsense girl. She cut me off and said simply, "He is a friend of Jerry's, so don't worry about being murdered. And on Monday morning, he goes abroad on work for almost two weeks and then you go to your parents' place for a week. This can't wait. You want to get married, right? This is the guy. I know it in my *kishkes*. He'll be at your building at 11 a.m."

Lapsed Catholic that she was, Paula loved using Yiddish words. Her pronunciation was better than mine. And we both knew that she had an excellent matchmaking record. And that my thirtieth birthday was just around the corner.

So Zack picked me up and we had brunch. And Paula was right. So right that I still can't believe it. Sitting across the table from him in a Starbucks, Paula found my soul mate.

He wasn't like the guys I'd been going out with. He had dark hair. He had a real job. He didn't jump out of airplanes or engage in extreme sports. In my prime, I could have drunk him under the table. But he was good-looking, smart, charming, and funny. And he swept me off my feet.

Did you guess that he was Jewish? I'm sure it had something to do with Paula's certainty that he was my soul mate.

That Sunday, we were together from 11 a.m. to 2 a.m. It was the best date I ever had, and I can't tell you how many I've been on. We spoke on the phone every day while he was in Europe and while I was with my parents. My mother knew something was up but had learned from experience not to ask. I decided that she deserved some good news from her only daughter and told her everything. I found a guy...and he was actually Jewish. She tried not to get excited but in her eyes, I saw joy and hope mixed with concern that maybe it wouldn't work out.

I would've married him by around 3 p.m. on the first date. But I played it cool. Dated normally. Never discussed marriage.

While we were dating, it became obvious that Zack was "more Jewish" than I was. He belonged to a shul, would never eat bacon or ham, and had been to Israel. I thought it was kind of quaint. My mother was thrilled.

The High Holidays came after we had been together for four months. They were important to him. Since I didn't know much about the holidays and my family didn't really celebrate them, we went to his parents' house. I'd met them before, but never for so much time. And the Jewish stuff was intimidating. But it was great. I loved his mom. And I loved the family coming together. And the traditional food. And the songs. I even liked the synagogue his family went to.

Towards the end of one of the meals, Zack leaned over and whispered to me, "I want this. Are you comfortable with all this? Can you do it?" It was the first time that he had ever referred to marriage so directly. "I love it," I replied. "I'll learn."

He didn't mention anything else about marriage for over two months. Should I bring it up? I didn't want to pressure him or seem desperate. But wasn't it obvious that this was "it"?

Paula came to the rescue, again. The three of us were walking out of a movie. Never one to mind her own business, in the middle of a monologue on the relative value of deodorant versus anti-perspirant, she turns to Zack and says, "If you don't ask her to marry you soon, you're crazy. How old do you want to be when you have kids?" She then turns to me and says, "And if you get neurotic and delay, I'll never set you up again."

I didn't know what to say. Zack couldn't stop staring at me.

The next day, he proposed. Six months later, we were married. Zack (and my mother) wanted a rabbi and a *chupah*. I would've been married by a frog if it would make Zack *and* my mother so happy, so of course I agreed. Since none of my friends were Jewish, I'd never even been to a Jewish wedding. I read a lot, and started to look forward to the ancient ceremonies and blessings that would add tradition and meaning to the beginning of our married lives. I walked around him seven times. He put the ring on my finger and broke the glass. It was the most beautiful wedding I'd ever been to.

A few months after the wedding, Zack brings home silver candlesticks that he got from his grandmother. Very elegant. "Grandma has an extra pair of these and I asked if maybe we could have them. She was thrilled. What do you think—do you want to use them?" he asked as he placed them in the middle of the shelf over the fake fireplace in our apartment.

I smiled and responded, "Of course." The next evening when he came home from work, a romantic dinner was waiting for him. I'd been cooking for hours and the place smelled great. The table was beautifully set. The wine was cooled. There were flowers. I was dressed up. And I'd bought beautiful candles and lit them in his grandmother's candlesticks, which I'd moved to the table.

It was Wednesday evening. Zack didn't say a word.

A few months later, we saw a movie that included a Jewish woman lighting candles on Friday afternoon before sunset. It clicked. They were Shabbat candlesticks and the point had been to light them and have a Friday night dinner. I cried, "Why didn't you tell me that's what you meant? How was I supposed to know? I feel so foolish."

But Zack said that he didn't want to pressure me in anything Jewish. He had an idea. The next Friday, I was out and came back only to shower and get dressed. He had left work a couple of hours early to prepare Shabbat dinner. I lit the candles. The meal was delicious. Best of all, we didn't go to a movie, show, or restaurant. We just sat at the table, enjoyed the wine and food, and talked. We also spent a lot of time just looking into each other's eyes.

The next weekend we went away with friends. It was nice but there were so many people, so much noise, and we were so busy that I didn't really feel we had much "quality time" together. I said so to Zack, who agreed.

So we did Friday night dinner again. And enjoyed it so much, we did it again and again until it became part of our lives. I look forward to it all week. I light the candles before sunset. We enjoy being in our home, dressing nicely, and drinking fine wine. We discuss anything and everything. Occasionally, we have guests. We laugh and tell stories. We share our dreams and fears. I even got Zack to sing with me occasionally. It has become our "sacred time."

I've also fallen in love with the holidays. We light the Chanukah candles together and talk about the miracle of Jewish survival. We clean the house for Passover, sing the Seder songs, and discuss freedom. We dip the apple in the honey on Rosh Hashanah and lovingly wish each other a sweet New Year.

The Jewish tradition is very marriage-oriented. I love the idea of what is called "*shalom bayit*," which means harmony in the home. Husbands and wives have as a primary goal to constantly work on their relationship. Traditionally, they even take classes and read books on the subject.

Several of my friends have confided in me that their marriages have not provided the close relationships they long for. They started out as in love and happy as Zack and I, but a few years later, they feel distant from their husbands.

Zack and I have such a huge advantage. We have a weekly time specifically created to help us focus on each other. We have wonderful holidays to look forward to together. We have a shared identity that deepens our bond. Being Jewish has added so much to our marriage. It is, I am convinced, the key to keeping our marriage as strong as it is.

Dear Diary
Judaism's effect on my family

I haven't written for over twenty years. You were once my closest confidante. With plenty of time at my disposal while I was a teenager, I would spend hours thinking and writing about my friends, the boys I liked, my parents and life in general. As I got older, I began living life instead of analyzing it. Yet tonight I feel there is something I must write down. If I try and talk about it too early, I'll start crying and not be able to continue. If I wait, I'm afraid that the freshness, depth, and intensity of my feelings will dissipate. So I've decided to put my thoughts on paper.

Today I went to synagogue. My husband, Jerry, and two children, Darren and Davie, go on most Saturday mornings. For me it was a rarity.

Jerry had grown up going to shul on Saturdays. He had stopped for a while in college and while single, but once we had kids, he wanted to go. I wasn't quite sure why. He talked about giving the kids a community and an identity. But I know it was deeper. Jerry felt very Jewish. And this was his way of expressing it.

Over the years, Jerry did try occasionally to encourage me to give shul a try, but he never pushed me. I never, ever, went. I simply wasn't interested. I didn't know when to stand up or sit down. I didn't know anyone there. Most of all, I didn't like the implications: I was happy with our lives. I didn't want to become "more Jewish."

So what changed? It has been a process, of course, but certain moments stick out. And they all have to do with the children. Last year, Darren came home and asked if we believe in Jesus. The hair on the back of my neck stood up. I wasn't prepared for his question. So I answered simply, "No, we don't."

"Why?"

"Because we're Jewish."

I found myself praying, actually praying, that Darren accepted the answer and didn't follow-up. But the years of encouraging independent thought and praising good questions had worked.

"But *why* don't Jews believe in Jesus?"

What would you answer? What do other people answer? I can't be the only Jewish parent who has had to deal with this stuff.

"Because Jesus is for Christians, honey. We're Jewish and he is not for us."

"Pete said that Jesus was a Jew who was the Messiah for everyone."

"Pete is wrong. We're Jews and Jesus is NOT for us." My answer, finally, seemed to have worked. Or not worked at all. Whatever the reason, he didn't ask any more questions.

The incident was over but not completely forgotten.

Santa Claus

A few months later was the holiday season. Chanukah had always been pretty minor in our house. Jerry lit the candles. I stood silently. I didn't make potato pancakes. I didn't buy the kids presents. We didn't sing songs or play dreidel.

The Christmas season, it seems, arrives a little earlier every year. That year, a week or two after Thanksgiving, the local mall already had a Santa Claus in full red gear promising kids presents. I tried to avoid him. But we were in the mall a lot and eventually the kids saw him.

"Can we go? This one gives you a treat, too. And you take a picture. Pete pulled his beard and said it was real…"

In previous years, I must admit, I'd let the kids go and sit on Santa's lap. I even have the pictures. After all, what's the harm? The kids were little and the whole set up is adorable.

But I had only a moment to decide. And, somehow, I had crystal clarity. We were bringing our kids up in an overwhelmingly non-Jewish area. They didn't go to Jewish school or even an afternoon religious school. We didn't practice Judaism at home. Our Chanukah celebration was quick and not particularly kid-friendly. If we—really, I—kept doing what we were doing, the kids might end up with no identity. Or they may join the Christian majority. But they were very unlikely to stay Jewish. They wouldn't know what it means. And they wouldn't care. And I knew then, from a place deep down inside of me, that I couldn't let that happen.

"No, kids. We have something even better. When you were little and couldn't understand I let you go to sit on his lap, but Santa is really for Christians. Chanukah is almost here and I want to do something special. Should we go choose Chanukah presents?"

That year, I made potato pancakes and the kids dunked them in applesauce. Each kid got a different (little) present each day. I got them each their own *menorah* and, under close supervision, they lit the candles themselves. Jerry taught me to sing "*hanerot halalu*" and "*maoz tzur.*" He and I sat down on the floor with the kids and played dreidel. The kids loved it. Jerry loved it. Although I had started the whole thing purely to fight Christmas, I loved it as well. I liked the family time. I liked the positive messages of the holiday.

Purim

A couple of months later, with a successful Chanukah behind us, Jerry felt emboldened and showed me a notice about the synagogue's Purim party. All I knew about Purim was that it was the Jewish Halloween. The notice mentioned the reading of the Scroll of Esther, a carnival for kids, and then a family meal. Interested, but hesitant, we went. Darren dressed up as a policeman, and Davie as a fireman. Jerry surprised me by borrowing a friend's surgical outfit. I dressed as me. The kids were told to use their noisemakers, stamp their feet, and boo whenever the wicked Haman's name was mentioned. They did, and were in their element. The carnival was full of fun booths and games. The meal was wonderful. Singing. Dancing. Drinking (for the adults, of course). The rabbi, dressed as a prisoner in black and white stripes, did a somersault and spent the day giving the kids rides on his shoulders. His wife, whom I met for the first time, was delightful. She was dressed as a huge butterfly and kept giving the children butterfly kisses. My kids were running around happily all day. Jerry was on cloud nine having me in shul. I was surprised by how many people there were very much like us. *The kind of people I'd like to be friends with*, I thought to myself.

Passover

Passover had always been a struggle in our family. Jerry wanted to have our own seders or go to his parents' house. I told him it was too much work to make our own and that I wanted to go to my parents' home. We both knew that his parents did a traditional seder while my folks didn't. Because they lived in different states and we couldn't do both in one year, we ended up arguing. One year we went to my parents' house and Jerry sulked the entire time. The next year, we went to his parent's house. I complained of a headache and skipped half the seder. Last year we went to Disneyworld instead of making Passover in order to avoid the issue.

What would happen this year? It was on my mind and I'm sure it was on Jerry's as well. In his usual careful way, he didn't say a word. But it was only a few weeks away. So I broached the subject.

"Can we talk about Passover?"

"Sure. Any ideas?"

"I don't want to fight and I don't want to skip it. I can't go to your parents. No offense. It is too much, their place is too small, and the expectations of me are too high. I can't do it. And my parents don't really do a full seder. And the kids are getting older and need more. But I can't make a seder. I don't know how…"

"I see you've thought through the possibilities. I agree with everything you said. We actually have local options. I was waiting for the right time to discuss it with you."

"Options? What options?"

"Eric and Jennifer invited us on the first night."

Eric was friend of Jerry's from shul. A shul buddy, as he said. Nice guy. Stockbroker. Normal. Jennifer was smart and funny and we had spent a lot of time talking on Purim. I had mentioned to Jerry that I liked her. They were very much like us, but did more Jewishly. Also, they had two boys that were the same ages as our boys. Good influences. It was a great match for our family, and we both knew it.

"Sounds good. What about the second night?"

"The rabbi invited us. Not just us. They have a few families and a bunch of singles, visitors, etc."

Jerry looked at me nervously. I'd never been in a rabbi's home, despite the occasional invitation. I shared my concerns.

"I don't know. It is a very nice thing to invite us. But it might be very long. They are very religious, you know. And it might all be in Hebrew. And we don't know all the rules..."

Jerry responded, "I know. I told him all that. And he told me to relax. Most of the people invited are similar to us, and he gears conversation towards our level of knowledge. Furthermore, the rabbi said, he doesn't really focus too much on the adults at all. It is all about the kids."

So, although nervous, I agreed to go.

Both nights exceeded our expectations.

We were Eric and Jennifer's only guests. The kids played nicely together and were ecstatic to be up so late. Jennifer and I got a lot closer. We read the entire *haggadah*, which was a first for me. They used props such as frogs and cotton balls to get the kids excited about the plagues. *We can do this*, I thought to myself. *This is nice.*

The rabbi and his wife made everyone, including me, feel very at home. He sat all the kids around him. And they loved the attention. Kids received a small chocolate for answering a question. For asking a question, they got two. Everyone got involved and told stories, acted things out, and had a great time. His own kids behaved so well and knew so much. *If I had grown up with seders like this, I'd never have left Judaism*, I thought to myself.

Saturday Morning

After Passover, we fell back into our regular routine. Until this morning. Jerry went to shul and I couldn't help thinking, "Why don't I go? He likes it. The kids like it. Even I like it. Good influences on my kids. Strengthens our friendships. Good community. Keeps the kids Jewish. What is so bad?"

So I got dressed quickly and caught up with Jerry and the kids on their way out. Davie gave me a hug. Darren had a huge smile and said, "Mommy! You're coming to shul?" Jerry took my hand silently. I had tears in my eyes. *This feels right*, I thought to myself, *this is what I want. For my family. And for me.*

Community
Where everybody knows your name

A friend of mine did an interesting experiment with her high school students. She promised them a special trip if they would each walk around with a button on their lapels, saying, "Hello. I am _____" with their first and last names spelled out. Some of the kids didn't want to do it. But there was a large group that agreed. School hours were relatively easy since people knew them anyway and other kids were wearing the same buttons. The hard part was on the way to school, after school, and the weekend. The teacher made it clear that they needed to wear the buttons the entire week, except for sleeping and showering.

The interesting thing is that my friend didn't tell anyone *why* they were wearing the pins. After the week was over, many of the kids who lasted through the entire week proudly announced their success. She told them about the fun excursion that she had arranged and they were excited. Then, in front of the whole class, the teacher asked the students if while wearing the pins they had acted any differently than usual. Slowly, one by one, each student realized and shared that indeed the buttons had caused them to act differently.

I was riding a bus and there was an old lady who got on. There wasn't a seat for her. I hate standing on a bus and don't ever get up for older people. But then I remembered that I was wearing my button. I was afraid that someone on the bus would know my parents and tell them that I had sat there while an old lady was left standing. So I got up and gave her my seat.

I was in the mall and a short distance away was a woman that works with my mother. She didn't recognize me since she only saw me once a long time ago, but I recognized her. She was having real trouble with her little boy. He was sitting on the ground and wouldn't move. He demanded to be picked up. The mother had a bunch of bags in her hands so that she couldn't possibly carry them and her son at the same time. I try to help people when I can but I was running late and wasn't going to help this time. Then I realized that I had my button on and if I helped, word would get back to my mother and it would make her very happy. So I walked over and helped her, making her and my mother very happy.

I wish that people were altruistic and kind and honest. And we are, sometimes. But the reality is that often the reason people do good things—or don't do bad things—is because others are watching.

This explains why many criminals are loners. They don't feel that they have to answer to anyone. Think about how we drive. Protected behind steel, I can cut people off. I can mouth insults to them. I'm anonymous. I don't have to answer for my actions.

The internet has had a similar effect. It has dramatically increased the number of people watching pornography. The same men passed X-rated shops and movie houses for years without ever venturing inside. So why are they suddenly watching so much pornography online? Because they were afraid to walk into the shops just in case they would be seen by someone and word would get back to their wives or girlfriends. Now they can watch from home when no one is around. No risk. They are anonymous.

At a simple level, therefore, one of the functions of community is to provide an external corrective when a person's internal sense of right and wrong gets cloudy. While there are few guarantees in life, community helps to keep people in line. We are not anonymous. If we act badly, we are likely to hear about it. This is a basic advantage of community, but it is not the only one.

Cheers: Where Everyone Knows Your Name

I grew up on a street in a typical middle class American suburb. Nice house, backyard, picket fence, dog. Like many people today, we didn't know people on our street. My parents never went out socially with any of our neighbors, and never visited their homes. The neighbors were never in our home. My brother and I each had our school friends and camp friends. And my parents had a few couples scattered around the city with whom they were close. But there was no sense of community in our lives.

We weren't alone. As Harvard Professor Robert Putnam details in his bestselling *Bowling Alone: The Collapse and Revival of American Community*, communal activities and rates of participation have dropped drastically over the last decades. Attendance at club meetings is down by fifty-eight percent, and at places of worship is down almost fifty percent. Over twenty percent of Americans move just about every year, and forty percent move every five years. Family dinners are down by over thirty-three percent, and even having friends come over for a visit is down by almost fifty percent. As the research indicates, effects of the waning of community are found in educational performance, safety on our streets, individual responsibility and integrity, personal health, and happiness. Most people have fewer and fewer close connections. And we need those connections, those relationships, dearly. Consider the following example.

Cat Love

A research team recently found that when pets (primarily puppies and kittens) are allowed in old age homes, the residents live longer and healthier lives. It is a sad statement that we need to import animal love to replace missing human affection.

But the report is also a useful demonstration that people need to be loved and to love. Healthy relationships, including both friends and family, are crucial to a person's overall state of happiness and self-esteem. And aside from its intrinsic importance, a person's mental state also has a huge impact on their physical health.

Baltimore

When I was sixteen, I spent two weeks with a friend at her home in the heart of Baltimore's Jewish community. I was shocked by how many people my friend's family knew. The adults knew their neighbors' kids' names, something that never happened on my street growing up. Neighbors knew each other and had real conversations. People from the community saw each other in synagogue on Saturday morning. When someone was sick, word got out and people came to visit and brought food. They invited each other to their family celebrations. I was amazed.

Years later, I began attending synagogue. One Saturday morning, a local family was hosting a *kiddush* to honor the birth of a baby daughter. The father stood up and said a few words. He talked about how great his wife is, how beautiful the baby is, and how they came to choose the baby's name. I don't remember much about this part of his talk. But then he said the following:

> *I want to thank you all for coming to share in our simchah. It means a lot to us and it is important. Let me explain why. Many of you will remember Mr. Goodman. He was the elderly man who lived in the blue house down the street and prayed here every morning. He was the first one in synagogue every morning. If you got up early to try and beat him, somehow he would be here first. He died a little over a year ago. He wasn't in shul one morning. It was the first time anyone could remember that he didn't come. So we called his apartment but there was no answer. We knocked on the door, but still no answer. So we called 911 and broke the door down. He had passed away*

> *during the night in his sleep. The community gave him a proper Jewish burial. That happened a year ago.*
>
> *Two nights ago, the police were also called to an apartment in town. About a ten minute drive from here. They were called because the neighbors were upset about a bad smell. The police knocked and phoned but there was no answer. Some neighbors had seen an old man living there, but no one knew his name. The police broke down the door. He had been dead for over 6 weeks. No one noticed.*

Being connected to other people, being part of a community, is vital. What is sad in the story above is not simply that the old man *died* alone in his apartment and no one noticed. What is sadder is that it seems that he *lived* alone in his apartment for years and no one noticed. He had no community.

Human beings are programmed to be social creatures. We need and crave companionship, including a life partner, friends, and community. When I realized how important community is, I thought about which community I wanted to join. And the Jewish community is impressive. It cares. It is involved. It is welcoming. It is both local and global. It is both immediate and historic. And it connects me to who I am, who I want to become, and to whom I want my kids to feel close. When I think of community, I think of my local Jewish community.

God Told Me to Be Jewish[1]
Indirect directions to stay Jewish

Don't worry. I didn't actually hear His voice. You can tell the men in the white suits to turn around and go back to whatever they were doing. They don't need to take me away. I'm normal. My brother Bernie doesn't think so, but he is twenty-three and listens to Barry Manilow music, so I'm not too worried about his opinions on normalcy.

What I mean by the title of this article is that over a number of years I came to the clear conclusion that being Jewish wasn't just fun, quaint, important, and cool (although it is all those things), but that I am supposed to be Jewish. I am meant to be Jewish. The cosmos destined it for me. God made it my destiny.

I can't fully explain to you the logic of the process I went through, because each step has books written about it and I only have a short article for all of them together (thanks a lot, editor!). Furthermore, part

---

[1] Names and identifying details have been changed where appropriate. The Indian Widows section is adapted from an article I wrote with Judy Auerbach in *Jewish Matters*. I am indebted to Lawrence Kelemen's *Permission to Believe* for his clear explanation of some of these ideas, which form the basis of part of this article.

of the process wasn't logical. I don't mean that it went against logic and reason, for it certainly didn't. I'm much too rational for that. What I mean is that in addition to the logical steps, part of me was directed by my gut. An inner, intuitive sense that this was right. "Right" as in morally right. And "right" as in true. The logical steps are vital, but my inner logic took me even further.

I want to try to describe at least some of the main realizations I had along the way. Keep in mind that your Jewish-identity process will likely be different from mine. I can only discuss what motivated me. Let us start at the beginning. Always a good place to start, as my mother says.

Step #1: Indian Widows

A number of years ago, a good friend recommended a book—a *New York Times* bestseller and a "classic." I tracked a copy down. It was called *The Closing of the American Mind*[2] by Professor Allan Bloom of the University of Chicago. I like beginning books from the end (another point for Bernie, I suppose). The deep German philosophy in the last chapters almost turned me off. But my internet connection was down and I was bored, so I actually flipped to the beginning of the book as well.

One experience Professor Bloom shared will remain permanently etched in my mind. I haven't seen it in a while, but this is the gist of it. He had taught philosophy for years, and every year he asked his freshman students what they would do in the following situation:

> *You are a British colonel in service to Her Majesty's army in India before they got independence there. You are touring the countryside when you notice a huge procession, sobbing and screaming. Quickly you realize it is a funeral procession. It seems a young man died tragically, and the whole village is attending the ceremony. Then you notice a young woman being led along to the funeral pyre. Villagers explain that as a widow, she will be burned alive—the custom in this part of the world.*

---

2 Simon & Schuster, 1988.

Then the professor would ask, "What do you do? Do you stop it? Do you want to stop it?" He would always get answers such as, "The British shouldn't have been there in the first place" or "It wasn't their country. What gives them the right to go there and tell others what to do?"

It seemed that tolerance of other cultures and mutual respect had gone so far as to convince many American students that there were no absolute rights and wrongs. Professor Bloom would declare himself an absolutist: There are some things that are absolutely, positively wrong, and I don't care whose culture is doing them. Murdering a healthy woman just because her husband died is simply wrong.

His students would look at him as if he were a Martian. The concept that "I do what I want, and you do what you want; you don't tell me how to live, and I don't tell you how to live" was fundamental to their identities. It had been pounded into their psyches consciously and subconsciously through school and the media. They had been taught that everything was relative: what is right for me is right for me, and what is right for you is right for you. We can't judge another culture or religion on the basis of *our* culture and religion. Professor Bloom used the Indian widow example to argue that there *were* indeed absolutes.

The first time I visited the Western Wall in Jerusalem I heard a similar idea. My tour guide sat us down somewhere and suggested that we find a few minutes to be alone. No cameras, no sharing impressions, no distractions. Just be alone and completely quiet. This was hard for us, who grew up with computers, televisions, answering machines, radios—we were not used to quiet. We were to close our eyes and look into ourselves. Our guide assured us that we would discover that inside we *did* believe there was meaning to life.

When I finally let myself do it (it took a while, I admit), I had a real moment of clarity. While I can't prove anything to you, there are certain things I *know* are wrong, and I know this with utmost certainty. I think most people agree with this. There are things that are just right and things that are just wrong.

Your objections can already be heard: Hitler! Stalin! Pol Pot! The Crusades! Look at what the idea of absolute truth has done to the world. Wars have been fought, millions of innocent people have died, and the world has been ravaged, all because of the idea that "what I believe is right; what you believe is wrong."

Okay, I agree that the concept can be abused. We'll get there—if I can bribe the editor with chocolate chip cookies into stretching the word limit. But for now, let us keep it simple. I know—and I mean *I know*—that there are some absolutes in the world. Murdering an innocent person who poses no immediate danger to others is simply wrong, no matter who does it or what excuse they give.

Step #2: Majority Rules?

Indians have a wonderful culture and heritage, but this aspect of it was plain wrong. Terrible, actually. But how do I know that I am right and they are wrong? The practice of *Sati* (also written *Suttee*) was widely practiced by many otherwise intelligent people until the British (largely) stamped it out. Maybe they were right? There are over a billion Indians and only one me!

No. That was the point that Professor Bloom was trying to make. *Suttee* was wrong no matter how many people believed in it.

Some will suggest that murder is wrong because, overall, the cultures and religions of the world have agreed to a certain number of unified principles. And murder is out of bounds for nearly all of them. Majority rule.

The only problem is that it isn't true. Most cultures and religions in the world's history have *not* condemned murder. Many were based on it: Greek and Roman societies regularly practiced infanticide.[3] Children who were deformed, sickly, or even those who had a minor defect were murdered or left to die. Often baby girls were killed because they were girls.

---

3   I am indebted to Rabbi Ken Spiro's *Worldperfect* for the information about ancient societies.

As Lloyd DeMause put it:

> *Infanticide during antiquity has usually been played down despite literally hundreds of clear references by ancient writers that it was an accepted, everyday occurrence. Children were thrown into rivers, flung into dung-heaps and cess trenches, 'potted' in jars to starve to death, and exposed in every hill and roadside, 'a prey for birds, food for wild beasts to rend' (Euripides, Ion, 504).*[4]

Plenty of physical evidence exists to this widespread practice of the ancient world. One well, the Athenian Agora, had the remains of 175 babies thrown inside to drown. This practice was justified by Aristotle[5] and most other ancient leaders and philosophers.[6] Of course, the cruelty to adults was even worse. Over 200 stadiums throughout the Empire were dedicated to watching innocent men, women, and children be mauled to death by starved animals or gladiators.

Today, it is true, the major cultures and religions of the world *do* condemn murder.

So maybe we know that murder is wrong because today most people realize it. We have progressed. But if this is the reason, what about fifty years from now? Or a hundred? If the majority of cultures and religions of the world declare murder legitimate, will they be right? Don't think it can't happen—in certain parts of the world, it *is* happening. Furthermore, was murder wrong a thousand years ago or not? If we judge by the majority culture at any given epoch, then was Roman brutality right? It can't be! Murder of innocents is murder!

Murder cannot be wrong because I say so or you say so. Or because we "know it." And this is for one simple reason: many, many others have said, do say, and will say differently.

---

4   *The Evolution of Childhood* (pp. 25-26).
5   "There must be a law that no imperfect or maimed child shall be brought up. And to avoid an excess in population, some children must be exposed. For a limit must be fixed to the population of the state" (Politics VII.16).
6   Seneca: "Children also, if weak and deformed, we drown, not through anger, but through the wisdom of preferring the sound to the useless" (*Concerning Anger*, I.XV).

So why *is* murder wrong?

Perhaps there is some "natural law" against it? The truth is otherwise, however. Nature is full of plants and animals killing others for their own benefit. Consider the weeds in my garden or carnivores in the animal world.

Perhaps murder is wrong because society breaks down when murder is accepted? But in many cases, like that of India above, society was not breaking down because of murder—in fact murder was a such a part of society that abolishing the practice caused more societal disruption than letting it continue!

If you think that the unnecessary murder of innocents is wrong—absolutely wrong—then it is not because of anything humans say and think, and not because of any natural laws or societal needs. If murder of innocents is wrong, it is only because there is a God Who made it wrong.[7]

As I realized that absolute morality means that God exists, I remembered Jimmy.

Step #3: The Big Bong

Jimmy was a sweet guy. Not too smart, but sweet. Both of these characteristics (not too smart and sweet) probably had to do with the fact that he was partially or fully stoned most of his adolescence. His parents were hippies from the sixties who grew, bought, and sold various illegal substances. His parents, and he, practically lived on the stuff.

I met him in college. Not his college—I don't think he finished high school—rather I was a student and he was the local...what is a polite way to say this...pusher. He supplied people from his family's garden. It was Vermont.

For the record, I never took up Jimmy's offer. For a thinking person, Jimmy was his own worst advertisement. No thanks.

---

[7] Interestingly, the Design Argument played little role in my development since for some reason I didn't think about it until years later. It is quite powerful. "If someone produced a copy of Tom Jones and claimed that nobody had written it, that it was a chance growth of wood curiously shaped and marked, I suppose he would encounter some incredulity. The universe being somewhat more intricate, beautiful, and impressive than Tom Jones..." Herman Wouk, *This Is My God,* epilogue, p. 230.

One thing he told me stood out in my mind, though. He once came over to me while I was sitting under a tree reading. He lay on the grass and said that his new batch was so good that he saw the universe being created, expanding and then contracting into nothingness...again and again and again.

> *God is breathing, man. I'm tapping into reality. Eternity. No beginnings and no endings. Just cosmic breathing—a never-ending cycle of creation and destruction. Eastern Karmic wisdom.*

Jimmy didn't seem to know much about reality, I admit, but was he right about the universe? Was it an endless cycle of expansion and contraction?

Beautiful idea, in a sense—an eternal rhythm to the universe. A living universe. The cosmic heart beating forever.

Poetic, but kind of fatalistic and depressing as well. Reminds me of a science fiction movie I once saw where humans look to an advanced alien race for explanations to life's deepest questions and keep getting told "this is how it is, this is how it always has been, and this is how it always must be." It was deep enough for me while I was laid out on my couch at 2 a.m. with a remote control in one hand and half eaten can of Pringles in the other. In retrospect, though, many years later, what kind of an answer is that? So if there are no beginnings and no endings, what is it all about? An endless cycle of life...for what? To keep living? Why? To improve the world only to see it destroyed, go back to barbarism, and improve it again? This is what all the pain and misery is about?

So I did a little research and it turns out that many scientists did indeed think that Jimmy was right...until the 1980's.

Let us start at the beginning. For many years, there were three models of the universe. Though many other names have been used, I refer to them as: (a) Boring Universe; (b) the Big Bong; and (c) the Big Bang.

The Boring Universe is usually known as the *static* model. In other words, the universe never changed. It was always in existence. If God exists at all, He really isn't that important in this model.

The Big Bong model is usually known as the *oscillating* model of the universe. Jimmy's drug-induced cosmic breathing model. In and out, expansion and contraction. Explosion sends everything out away from the center and gravity eventually pulls everything back into the center. And again and again. No need for God in this model either.

The Big Bang model is similar except that the explosion only happened once. Not enough gravity to pull all matter back towards the center. This "open" universe will eventually burn out and spread out into nothingness. A few questions stand out at this idea, though: If there was only one initial explosion, how did it start? This model seems to suggest that an external actor, i.e. God, actually got things rolling.

For centuries, these three models vied for supremacy and each has its advocates. No more. In 1925, Edwin Hubble discovered that every galaxy is receding away from the center. In 1965, Arno Penzias and Robert Wilson discovered cosmic microwave background radiation from a huge explosion at the beginning of the universe. They were awarded Nobel prizes for their discovery. Combined with Hubble's work, The Boring (static) model was dead. The universe was not static. It had started with an explosion, and the various galaxies thus created are still moving away from the original central point of the Big Bang.

But perhaps the explosion was only one of many in an endless cycle of cosmic breathing, expansion, and contraction? Which was right—the Big Bang or the Big Bong?

Dr. Robert Jastrow was for many years head of NASA's Goddard Institute for Space Studies, and one of the leading physicists and astronomers in the world. He and many others studied—for years—the amount of matter in the universe to determine if indeed it was sufficient to produce enough gravity to cause a contraction. In 1978, he declared that the entire weight of matter in the universe is "still more than ten times too small to bring the expansion...to a halt."[8] This was big news in the 1970's but by now is common knowledge. There have

---

8   Jastrow, *Have Astronomers Found God?* New York Times Magazine, 25 June 1978.

been no endless contractions and expansions. The Big Bong theory was incorrect. The Big Bang theory is the only fighter left in the ring.

Indeed, the universe had a beginning. Creation Ex Nihilo. Something from nothing. And the implications were clear to Dr. Jastrow:

> *This religious faith of the scientist is violated by the discovery that the world had a beginning under conditions in which the known laws of physics are not valid, and as a product of forces or circumstances we cannot discover. When that happens, the scientist has lost control...*
>
> *Consider the enormity of the problem. Science has proven that the universe exploded into being at a certain moment. It asks what cause produced the effect? Who or what put the matter and energy in the universe? Was the universe created out of nothing, or was it gathered together out of pre-existing materials? And science cannot answer these questions.*
>
> *...For the scientist who has lived by his faith in the power of reason, the story ends like a bad dream. He has scaled the mountain of ignorance; he is about to conquer the highest peak; as he pulls himself over the final rock, he is greeted by a band of theologians who have been sitting there for centuries.*[9]

Contemplating this, I became more comfortable with the idea that there was indeed an absolute morality, and that it could only be absolute if we brought God into the picture. Scientists can explain much from the Big Bang on, but cannot explain how it started on its own, contrary to all basic laws of physics.

So it made sense to me that God had created the world and somehow given us some rules of absolute morality. But what happened since then? Did He just get up and walk away?

---

9   Robert Jastrow, *God and the Astronomers*, quoted on http://en.wikiquote.org/wiki/Judaism.

Step #4: Is God Dead?

Carlsbad Caverns National Park in Southeast New Mexico. I don't know if you like caves, but this one is impressive. Six football fields large, incredible rock formations. You feel like you're in the temple from the last Matrix film, minus Morpheus. I'm following around the tour guide. Outwardly, I'm just another tourist. Inside, I'm struggling over the implications of the death of Jimmy's Big Bong theory, as described above. So when the guy in front of me says, "Wow. Mother Nature knew what she was doing!" something from inside of me—me, the person who has never even thought anything remotely spiritual in my entire life, and certainly never said it out loud—responds, "God gave us a present."

My fellow tourist didn't take my comment well and responded testily, "Well I think He is pretty busy up there and doesn't get involved in caves..."

End of that conversation.

I realized that I should have just minded my own business. But my main thought was:

> *You, sir, are an idiot. Either there is a God or there isn't. If you don't think there is one, fine. Your life. But don't say things that are so patently absurd. God is God. He does not get "busy" with the Milky Way and does not have the time, mental energy, or budget to complete the other galaxy that He promised to finish by next Tuesday. I still can't rub my tummy and pat my head at the same time. He can (so to speak).*

God is unlimited and all-powerful. He is God. He doesn't "go away." He doesn't create things and then get bored with them and move on to other projects He is still around, and paying attention.

Step #5: God's Guidance

The realization that God is still around also answered a deeper and more practical concern—God *must* have given us some kind of instructions for life.

If you were God, wouldn't you?

Think about it. God is perfect. Knows everything and can do whatever He wants. Sounds a little like my mother. But back to our subject: God. He didn't *need* to create the world. He wasn't lacking anything. He wasn't lonely. He wasn't sad. All these attributes are human ones that simply don't apply. God is, was, and always will be perfect. It is one of the few things that we can say about Him. So making the world was not for His benefit. It was for ours.

But what are we supposed to do here? Is a *Lord of the Flies* life what He wanted for us? How about a murdering-widows-in-India life? Or a Nazi-life (they almost won, remember) or a Pol Pot life?

He couldn't have meant any of this. But if He never gave us any instructions, how are we supposed to know what we are here for?

If I were God, I would certainly have revealed myself—excuse me, I mean Myself—and given some indication of what life is all about.

Step #6: The Miracle of the Jews

Notice that up until now, the previous five steps were essentially universal. They have to do with meaning, right and wrong, God, and the idea that if God exists, He must have created us for something and given us an indication of what life is about and what He wants. During the months (years?) that I was struggling with these five steps (obviously in greater detail than the notes I've penned above), I hadn't yet really considered anything Jewish. But my thinking about meaning, God, and destiny got me thinking about my Jewish heritage. And with the help of a few books and lot of time online, I came face to face with the incredible miracle of the Jewish People, sometimes called the "wonder" of the Jewish People.[10]

Approximately 3000 years ago, the Book of Books, a.k.a. the Bible, a.k.a. the Torah, said some incredible things about the Jews. It described how the Jewish People was supposed to be a unique People with a unique message throughout the generations. A Kingdom of Priests and a Holy Nation. Traditional dating has the Torah written around

---

10   This part of the article is partially inspired by the Discovery Seminar as well as the publications and teachings of Arachim, and articles on simpletoremember.com.

1300 BCE. Some scholars and critics claim that it, or parts of it, were actually written later, around 800 BCE. I'm convinced that their view is mistaken for many reasons, but for our purposes here, it makes no difference. The Torah predicted the history of the Jewish People way before there was a history of the Jewish People.

Let us look at what the Bible actually said would happen to the Jews. We're going to focus on six points: (a) we will be exiled from Israel and dispersed throughout the world; (b) we will always have a small population; (c) anti-Semitism will follow us; (d) despite these great difficulties, the Jews will be an eternal Nation; (e) we will be a light to the nations; and (f) we will return to Israel.

Exile and Dispersion

Way before we had ever been exiled at all, the Torah declared:[11]

> "And you, I will scatter among the nations, at the point of My drawn sword, leaving your country desolate and your cities in ruins."
>
> Leviticus 26:33.

Only a handful of nations have ever been completely exiled from their own land. And in almost all of those cases, the nation is exiled, assimilates, and is never heard from again. Furthermore, no other people has been scattered like the Jews. In their epic struggle to survive, Jews have gone anywhere and everywhere they could. We were first exiled from our own land in 586 BCE and sent to Babylon. After seventy years, we returned to Israel and were exiled by the Romans in seventy CE—ending up all over the world. No other nation has ever returned to its own land after being exiled, let alone be exiled again. Our exile and dispersion are indeed remarkable[12] when seen in an historical context—exile has been such a part of our history that we are called "wandering Jews."

---

11 Consider also Deut. 4:26-27 and Ezek. 12:11-15, 22:15.
12 "When we scan the Diaspora of Jewry over the entire globe and throughout the entire civilized world, we are surprised to see that this Nation, which is almost the most ancient in the world, is in truth the youngest in terms of the land under its feet and the sky above

Small Population

"God will then scatter you among the nations, and only a small number will remain among the nations where God shall lead you."[13]

Deuteronomy 4:27

Other nations' populations (such as the Chinese and Indians, as only two examples) have increased exponentially over the centuries. The Jews presently comprise twelve to fourteen million people, roughly the same number we had at the end of the Holocaust, and not much more than we had throughout the centuries. Despite our tradition's focus on the family, our numbers have not gone up significantly.

Continual Presence of Anti-Semitism

There has always been racism. And sexism. And other *isms*. Sadly, they are slow to disappear. Yet there is only one people who, due to the unique and powerful hatred of it, actually has its own word to describe this vicious phenomenon. The Jews win this dubious award and the word is anti-Semitism.

Anti-Semitism has been more vicious, more consistent, and more common than most people realize. No other hatred even begins to match its intensity and longevity:

> ...As my research into Jewish history progressed, I was surprised, depressed, and to some extent overwhelmed by the perpetual and irrational violence which pursued the Jews in every country and to almost every corner of the globe. If, therefore, persecution, expulsion, torture, humiliation, and

---

its head. As a result of the relentless persecutions and forced expulsions, most Jews are but recent newcomers to their respective lands of residence. Ninety percent of the Jewish People have lived in their new homes for no more than fifty or sixty years! [The Jewish People] are dispersed throughout over 100 lands on all five continents" (A. Leschzinsky, *The Jewish Dispersion*, p. 9 [Heb.]).

13   See also Deut. 28:62.

mass murder haunt these pages, it is because they also haunt the Jewish story.

(Sir) Martin Gilbert, "Jewish History Atlas" Oxford 1985

In almost every generation over thousands of years, Jews have been the subjects of forced conversions, expulsions, pogroms, riots, burnings, and other attacks somewhere around the world.[14] The universality and intensity of anti-Semitism has attracted much notice. Perhaps even more important is its inherent irrationality:

Of all the extreme fanaticism that plays havoc in man's nature, there is none as irrational as anti-Semitism. The Jews cannot vindicate themselves in the eyes of these fanatics. If the Jews are rich, they are victims of theft and extortion. If they are poor, they are victims of ridicule. If they take sides in a war, it is because they wish to gain advantage from the spilling of non-Jewish blood. If they espouse peace, it is because they are scared and anxious by nature or traitors to their country. If the Jew dwells in a foreign land, he is persecuted and expelled. If he wishes to return to his own land, he is prevented from doing so.

British Prime Minister Lloyd George[15]

Historically speaking, it matters little what the Jews say or do. They are hated. As Professor Michael Curtis of Rutgers University put it:

The uniqueness of anti-Semitism lies in the fact that no other people in the world have ever been charged simultaneously with alienation from society and with cosmopolitanism, with being capitalistic exploiters and also revolutionary communist advocators. The Jews were accused of having an imperious mentality; at the same time they're a People of the Book. They're accused of being militant aggressors, at the same time as being cowardly pacifists. With being a Chosen People, and

---

14 Some of this section is inspired by material at simpletoremember.com
15 Stated in 1923

also having an inferior human nature. With both arrogance and timidity. With both extreme individualism and community adherence. With being guilty of the crucifixion of Jesus and at the same time held to account for the invention of Christianity.[16]

It is startling to read that the Bible predicted anti-Semitism thousands of years before its appearance:

Among those nations you shall find no respite, no rest for your foot. There God will make you cowardly, destroying your outlook and making life hopeless. You will live in constant suspense. Day and night, you will be terrified, never sure of your existence. In the morning you will say, "If only it were night," and in the evening you will say, "If only it were morning!" Such will be the dread that your heart will feel and the sights that your eyes will see."

Deuteronomy 28:65-67

Eternal Nation

We were faced with the seemingly insurmountable obstacles of exile, dispersion, small numbers, and continual persecution and anti-Semitism. Yet despite these unique challenges, we are still here to talk about it.

Over 3,500 years ago, God promised Abraham that his descendants, the Jews, will be an eternal nation:

And I will establish My covenant between Me and you, and your descendants after you, throughout the generations. An eternal covenant to be your God, and the God of your descendants after you."[17]

Genesis 17:7

---

16   Colloquium on anti-Semitism, 1987.
17   Similar ideas appear in Leviticus 26:43, Deuteronomy 4:26-27, Deuteronomy 28:63-64, Isaiah 54:10, Jeremiah 31:34-35 and more.

And, incredibly, we are still going strong. There are indeed other peoples who can trace themselves back to similar periods of time, notably the Chinese and Indians, but the similarities stop there. The Chinese and Indians of today bear little resemblance to the people of the ancient world. Their language is different. Their religion is vastly different and, perhaps most importantly, massive migrations throughout the ages have made it unlikely that many of the people living in those countries today are actually the physical descendants of the ancient Chinese and Indians.[18]

The incredible survival of the Jews has been noticed by many non-Jewish historians and thinkers. Consider these comments:

> *The Egyptian, Babylonian, and the Persian rose, filled the planet with sound and splendor, then faded to dream-stuff and passed away. The Greek and Roman followed, made a vast noise, and they are gone. Other peoples have sprung up, and held their torch high for a time, but it burned out and they sit in twilight now or have vanished. The Jew saw them all, beat them all, and is now what he always was, exhibiting no decadence, no infirmities of age, no weakening of his parts, no slowing of his energies, no dulling of his alert and aggressive mind. All things are mortal, but the Jew. All other forces pass, but he remains. What is the secret of his immortality?*
>
> Mark Twain[19]

The more one looks into the survival of the Jewish People, the more incredible it becomes. If history was a competition for survival, others had innumerable advantages over the Jews: they had their own land, they had power, they had self-control. We were powerless and persecuted. Other peoples should have won the race and we should be a footnote in the history books. Yet, defying all natural and historical laws, we have outlived them all:

---

18 Wikipedia articles on China and India are a good starting point on these massive migrations.
19 *Concerning the Jews*, Harper's Magazine, March 1898.

The preservation of the Jews is really one of the most signal and illustrious acts of Divine Providence...and what but a supernatural power could have preserved them in such a manner as none other nation upon earth hath been preserved. Nor is the providence of God less remarkable in the destruction of their enemies, than in their preservation...We see that the great empires, which in their turn subdued and oppressed the People of God, are all come to ruin...And if such hath been the fatal end of the enemies and oppressors of the Jews, let it serve as a warning to all those, who at any time or upon any occasion are for raising a clamor and persecution against them.

Thomas Newton, Bishop of Bristol[20]

This People are not eminent solely by their antiquity, but are also singular by their duration, which has always continued from their origin till now. For, whereas the nations of Greece and of Italy, of Lacedaemon, of Athens and of Rome, and others who came long after, have long since perished, these ever remain, and in spite of the endeavors of many powerful kings who have a hundred times tried to destroy them, as their historians testify, and as it is easy to conjecture from the natural order of things during so long a space of years, they have nevertheless been preserved (and this preservation has been foretold); and extending from the earliest times to the latest, their history comprehends in its duration all our histories (which it preceded by a long time).

Blaise Pascal[21]

The preservation of the Jew was certainly not casual. He has endured through the power of a certain ideal, based on the recognition of a Higher Power in human affairs. Time after

---

20 1704-1782.
21 Pensees by Blaise Pascal (1623-1662) Encyclopedia Britannica, 1952—para. 620, p. 285.

> time in his history, moreover, he has been saved from disaster in a manner, which cannot be described excepting as 'providential.' The author has deliberately attempted to write this book in a secular spirit; he does not think that his readers can fail to see in it, on every page, a higher immanence.
>
> Professor Cecil Roth of Oxford[22]

Light Unto the Nations

Surviving the unique challenges of exile and anti-Semitism persecution is miraculous enough, as noted by the many non-Jewish thinkers quoted above. But what is even more astounding is that a small, persecuted nation like the Jews could have such a major impact on the world:

Consider these comments by non-Jewish thinkers and observers:

> He is as prominent on the planet as any other people, and his commercial importance is extravagantly out of proportion to the smallness of his bulk. His contributions to the world's list of great names in literature, science, art, music, finance, medicine, and abstruse learning, are also way out of proportion to the weakness of his numbers.
>
> Mark Twain[23]

> The Jews started it all—and by "it" I mean so many of the things we care about, the underlying values that make all of us, Jew and Gentile, believer and atheist, tick. Without the Jews, we would see the world through different eyes, hear with different ears, even feel with different feelings...we would think with a different mind, interpret all our experience differently,

---

22 *History of the Jews*, New York, 1963, p. 424.
23 Ibid.

*draw different conclusions from the things that befall us. And we would set a different course for our lives.*²⁴

Thomas Cahill, The Gifts of the Jews

*Asked to make a list of the men who have most dominated the thinking of the modern world, many educated people would name Freud, Einstein, Marx, and Darwin. Of these four, only Darwin was not Jewish. In a world where Jews are only a tiny percentage of the population, what is the secret of the disproportionate importance the Jews have had in the history of Western culture?*²⁵

Ernest van den Haag, The Jewish Mystique²⁶

Jewish and non-Jewish thinkers throughout history have marveled at the Jewish impact on the world in so many areas. Even more startling, perhaps, is the fact that the Bible itself clearly predicted this:

I will make you into a great Nation. I will bless you and make your name great. You shall become a blessing. And I will bless those who bless you, and curse those who curse you. Through you all the communities of the earth shall be blessed.

Genesis 12:2-3²⁷

---

24   Similarly: "If we were forced to choose just one, there would be no way to deny that Judaism is the most important intellectual development in human history" (David Gelernter, Yale University Professor).
25   Similarly: "The brief legal emancipation of Jews during the Napoleonic wars released unparalleled economic, professional, and cultural energies. It was though a high dam had suddenly been breached" (Amos Elon, *The Pity of It All—A portrait of the German-Jewish Epoch 1743-1933* [New York: Picador, 2002], p. 6).
26   New York: Dell Publishing Company, 1971, p. 13.
27   Consider also: "Now, if you obey Me and keep My covenant, then you shall be My special treasure among all the nations, for all the world is Mine. And you will be a Kingdom of Priests and a Holy Nation to Me…(Exodus 19:5-6)."

> And I will establish you as a covenant of the people, for a light unto the nations.
>
> Isaiah 42:6

The Return

Three thousand years ago, the Bible promised our exile. But it also promised our return:

> The Almighty will bring back your captivity and have mercy upon you; and He will return and gather you from among all of the nations where He has dispersed you. If your dispersed ones will be even at the ends of the Heavens, from there God Almighty will gather you and from there He will take you. And the Lord your God will bring you to the Land that your fathers inherited and you shall inherit it and He will do good for you and make you more numerous than your forefathers.
>
> Deuteronomy 30:1-5[28]

And return we have. 200 years ago, only a few hundred Jews lived in Israel. One hundred years ago, the Jewish population was in the thousands. Now there are over six million Jewish citizens of Israel, making it the single largest Jewish population in the world.

No other people has ever returned to a land they were exiled from, let alone after 2000 years. The Jewish People's return to Israel is one of the great miracles of history.

Step #7: Destiny

There are many reasons for being Jewish. It is a wonderful way of life. It connects a person to God and spirituality. It is an important tradition that changed the planet and is crucial to the planet's future. History has shown that the Jews have a central role to play in bringing about a better future, free of war and conflict, and full of spirituality. These are all good reasons to stay Jewish and there are many reasons like them.

---

28 See also Isaiah 49:18-22, Jeremiah 31:6-7, and Jeremiah 33:10-11.

What I have focused on here is my personal experience and realization that there is another reason. A powerful reason that convinced me that God wants me to stay Jewish. Every person will approach things differently. I have shared my basic path, step by step:

I know there are absolute rights and wrongs. These can only exist if there is a God. If God is God, He is ever-present and wants us to live lives of meaning. He did not abandon the world He created. He gave us guidance. And when I looked in history for evidence of His guidance, the story of the Jewish People entranced me. A People of miracles. A People that was exiled more than any other people and persecuted more than any other people and yet survived longer than any other people. And not only survived but had a most startling and unparalleled impact on the world: contributions in every field of human endeavor and especially in the most central areas of morality and spirituality. And a People that returned to its Land in a feat unparalleled in history.

All these are miracles. But the greatest miracle of all is that these feats were clearly predicted thousands of years ago in the Book of Books, the Bible, hundreds and thousands of years before they actually occurred.

My conclusion was and is clear. God made the world. He made me Jewish. And He wants me to stay Jewish.

Tolstoy and Me
Jewish inspiration from the greatest Russian ever

I'm not quite sure exactly when my obsession started.

Perhaps it goes back to the Russian cleaning lady who used to work for us when I was five years old. She secretly gave me treats from the "out-of-bounds" drawer when Mom wasn't around.

Or, perhaps, my interest dates from my beloved Russian grandfather. I loved my other grandparents, of course, but they were more American, and thus less interesting.

Zeyde Abie, as we called him, always had a joke and a story for the kids. It is hard not to love someone who loves you and makes you laugh. And of course, when he was gone I missed him terribly.

Or, perhaps, it was the Free Russian Jewry movement from the 1970s that did it. Russian Jews were oppressed for the great sin of being Jewish. If they dared to learn Hebrew, keep Jewish rituals, or apply to move to Israel, they would usually have the KGB (secret police) on their tails, lose their jobs, and even end up in jail. Some Soviet Jews languished for many years. My uncle Mark was active in the action committees, which ultimately helped get the Russians to let the Jews go. He brought me to several demonstrations and even to a March on Washington where I remember shouting, "Let My People Go!"

Or maybe it was a taste for the exotic. I grew up in the Cold War. The Russians were hard-line Communists. It was an evil regime. No freedom of speech. No freedom of religion. No freedom of any kind, really. It was a dark, closed society that put men in prison—and into space. It developed incredible literature—and a powerful, aggressive military. And, my father said, made the best darn vodka in history. Fascinating, different, and enticing to a young boy.

All of these, I'm sure, played a part and reinforced my interest in Russian culture and literature. Nevertheless, if I had to choose one thing to explain my Russian fixation, it would be Tolstoy. We were assigned *War and Peace* to read in high school. Many of the other kids hated it, found it boring, and relied on Cliff's notes to write their book report. I, on the other hand, feigned a fever in order to be able to stay at home in bed and keep reading. I fell in love. Surprising result for a teenage boy, I know, but something about the cadence, the breadth of history, and the imagery made my heart sing.

I went to the library to get more Tolstoy works. The librarian said with a smile, "Too bad you can't read Russian—translations are so limited."

What? You mean that the most moving thing ever written was really only a poor copy of the original? It was like hearing that your favorite food, the one you would gladly eat every meal if your mother let, is actually prepared much better at a restaurant down the street. What would you do?

Learn Russian, of course. Since learning a language was obligatory and my interest in French was very low (desolé, mes amis!), switching to Russian seemed like a great idea. I worked hard at it. Within two years, I was reading Tolstoy's works in the original. (Amazing what we can achieve when we want something.) The librarian was right—Tolstoy's use of the Russian language was magical. Of course, I also read Pushkin, Gogol, and Dostoevsky, but for me at least, Tolstoy was the center of all things Russian. He was undoubtedly the greatest living Russian of his time. A nobleman turned writer turned philosopher turned anarchist. Isaak Babel commented, "If the world could write by itself, it would write like Tolstoy." Virginia Woolf described him as the "greatest of all novelists," and Gandhi openly acknowledged the tremendous influence

Tolstoy had on his own thinking, declaring in his autobiography that Tolstoy was "the greatest apostle of non-violence that the present age has produced."

Agree with him or not, Lev Nikolayevich Tolstoy was no lightweight. Imagine my shock when I, young Russian-loving Jew that I was, came across the following words written by Tolstoy towards the end of his life.

> *What is a Jew? This question is not at all so odd as it seems. Let us see what kind of peculiar creature the Jew is, which all the rulers and all the nations have together and separately abused and molested, oppressed and persecuted, trampled and butchered, burned and hanged...and in spite of all this is yet alive.*
>
> *What is a Jew, who has never allowed himself to be led astray by all the earthly possessions which his oppressors and persecutors constantly offered him in order that he should change his faith and forsake his own Jewish religion?*
>
> *The Jew is that sacred being who has brought down from the heaven the everlasting fire and has illuminated with it the entire world. He is the religious source, spring, and fountain out of which all the rest of the peoples have drawn their beliefs and their religions.*
>
> *...The Jew is the emblem of eternity. He whom neither slaughter nor torture of thousands of years could destroy, he whom neither fire nor sword nor inquisition was able to wipe off the face of the earth, he who was the first to produce the Oracles of God, he who has been for so long the guardian of the prophecy, and who transmitted it to the rest of the world—such a nation cannot be destroyed. The Jew is as everlasting as is eternity itself.*[1]

To say I was in shock would be the understatement of the year. Here was my hero, my Russian hero, whose language I had learned, whose

---

[1] *What is a Jew?* Leo Nikolaivitch Tolstoy, Jewish World periodical, London 1908.

culture I had admired, whose writings and opinions were, literally, worshipped by Russian society as a whole, and whom was he impressed by? By the Jews. By me.

Until this point, being Jewish was a non-issue in my life. Of course, I had a bar mitzvah (Disco theme. What else needs to be said?) and did some synagogue Sunday school. But my parents went to shul only twice a year (arriving late and leaving early on both occasions, mind you) and didn't really know or care much themselves. Aside from my uncle Mark (of "Let My People Go" fame, see above), Jewishness was a low priority in our lives. Being Jewish didn't seem either special or important. Until Tolstoy told me that it was both.

When we hear something from an insider, we know the evaluation is not objective. Growing up, my mother would tell me on a daily basis that I was the cutest and smartest child alive. Good for the ego, perhaps, but far from the truth. When the Pope tells you how great Catholicism is, I'm not impressed. He is paid to think that—he is the Pope. But when an outsider—and a very impressive one at that—wrote passionately about the greatness of the Jews, I took notice. Did anyone else feel that way, or was Tolstoy alone? One visit to the library enabled me to quickly find many similar comments, from some of the most astute thinkers, activists, and writers that the world has produced.

Consider the words of Mark Twain:

> *If the statistics are right, the Jews constitute but one percent of the human race. It suggests a nebulous dim puff of stardust lost in the blaze of the Milky Way. Properly the Jew ought hardly to be heard of; but he is heard of, has always been heard of. He is as prominent on the planet as any other people, and his commercial importance is extravagantly out of proportion to the smallness of his bulk. His contributions to the world's list of great nations in literature, science, art, music, finance, medicine, and abstruse learning, are also way out of proportion to the weakness of his numbers. He has made a marvelous fight*

118   Why Be Jewish?

in this world, in all the ages; and has done it with his hands tied behind him. He could be vain of himself, and be excused for it.²

Consider also the words of John Adams, second president of the United States:

> I will insist that the Hebrews have done more to civilize men than any other nation. If I were an atheist and believed in blind eternal fate, I should still believe that fate had ordained the Jews to be the most essential instrument for civilizing the nations...They are the most glorious Nation that ever inhabited this Earth. The Romans and their empire were but a bauble in comparison to the Jews. They have given religion to three quarters of the globe and have influenced the affairs of mankind more, and more happily than any other nation, ancient or modern.³

It is said that King Louis XIV of France asked the great philosopher Pascal for some proof of a supernatural force in the world. "Why the Jews, your majesty," Pascal answered. "The Jews."

Awe of the survival, contributions, and centrality of the Jews continues into our time as well. Contemporary (non-Jewish) historian Paul Johnson wrote:

> All the great conceptual discoveries of the intellect seem obvious and inescapable once they have been revealed, but it requires a special genius to formulate them for the first time.
>
> The Jews had this gift. To them we owe the idea of equality before the law, both divine and human, of the sanctity of life and the dignity of the human person, of the individual conscience and so of personal redemption; of the collective conscience and so of social responsibility; of peace as an abstract ideal

---

2   *Concerning the Jews*, Mark Twain, Harpers Magazine, 1899. Republished in *The Complete Essays of Mark Twain* (Doubleday, 1963), p. 249.

3   *On the Jews*, John Adams, second president of the United States, from a letter to F.A. Van der Kemp, February 16, 1806, Pennsylvania Historical Society.

*and love as the foundation of justice, and many other items which constitute the basic moral furniture of the human mind. Without the Jews, it might have been a much emptier place.*⁴

The interesting thing is that when one looks at the writings of anti-Semites, they often feel that our impact has been even greater! Consider these words of Adolf Hitler:

*The struggle for world domination will be fought entirely between us, between Germans and Jews. All else is facade and illusion. Behind England stands Israel, and behind France, and behind the United States. Even when we have driven the Jew out of Germany, he remains our world enemy.*⁵

Hitler vastly overemphasized Jewish power. But he did understand our role in the world, as he said: *Conscience is a Jewish invention; it is a blemish like circumcision.*⁶

Have you ever gone through a paradigm shift?

Imagine living many years believing you wanted to be a lawyer. You were destined to be a lawyer. All the classes and activities you took in high school and as an undergrad were focused on getting into the best law school. You got in and excelled. You graduate, start practicing, and then within a few months come to the sudden but crystal-clear conclusion that you hate everything about law. At first, you deny the new feelings and keep doing what you are doing. That doesn't work. So you attempt to change fields within law, to try different clients, methods, and goals. Still, after several changes, the conclusion is undeniable. Being a lawyer simply isn't you, and you have to re-evaluate your life.

This is what I went through in the days and weeks that followed the Tolstoy revelation about the Jewish People. What was Russian literature, after all? Beautiful it certainly is, but in my heart of hearts I knew there was plenty of beauty elsewhere as well. And what did Tolstoy and

---

4   *A History of the Jews*, Paul Johnson (HarperCollins, New York, 1987), p. 585.
5   Rauschning, *Hitler Speaks*, p. 234.
6   Ibid., p. 220.

other greats see in the Jewish narrative that I had never even noticed? And of course, there was the nagging question I wanted to ask but was afraid of: What *was* the Jewish narrative, anyway? What was Judaism all about? I knew so little.

So I started looking into my Jewish identity. I read books. I went to Torah classes. I traveled to Israel. I was fascinated by the Jewish enigma. As eminent sociologist Milton Himmelfarb put it, "The number of Jews in the world is smaller than a small statistical error in the Chinese census. Yet we remain bigger than our numbers. Big things seem to happen around us and to us."

They certainly did. And do. Russian literature is still impressive, but it is someone else's narrative. I became interested in my story. In *our* story. The Hebrews. The Israelites. The magical People of Israel. The Jews.

Appendix I
Nobel Prize Winners[1]

The Jewish contribution to the world is simply amazing. Jews currently make up 0.21 percent of the world's population, yet account for at least 21.19 percent[2] of all Nobel prize recipients worldwide between 1901 and 2007. Included in this list are recipients who are clearly Jewish. Many other candidates' origins are likely Jewish but are not included here due to the lack of certainty—many observers are convinced that the actual percentage of Jewish prizewinners is significantly higher.

---

1 Nobel prizes are perhaps the best, but not the only, indication of the incredible Jewish contribution to the world. Dozens of Web sites compile Jewish achievements in science, culture, etc. Do an internet search for up-to-date information that interests you. Here are a few more examples: Jews have received 74 percent of Tony awards for Best Original Score of a Musical, 67 percent for Best Musical Production and 44 percent of Best Play awards, as well as 53 percent of Academy Awards for Best Original Song and 51 percent for Best Musical Scoring of a Motion Picture. In addition, 52 percent of all recipients of the Pulitzer Prize for Non-Fiction have been Jewish, as well as 35 percent of those for Drama. From 1886 to 2000, Jews accounted for 54 percent of World Chess Champions and wrote 42 of the 50 most cited works in Arts & Humanities Literature. Also, 39 of "The 100 Most Eminent Psychologists of the 20th Century" were Jewish.

2 In the fields of chemistry, economics, medicine, and physics, the number is 27 percent.

Some winners are well-known, many are not. The point of listing them here is to encourage us to spend a moment and contemplate: how can such a small People, persecuted, exiled and maligned, accomplish so much? Our contributions are an incredible achievement and without any historic parallel.[3]

Jewish Nobel Prize Winners in Medicine (49 out of 189)

2006	Andrew Z. Fire for the "discovery of RNA interference—gene silencing by double-stranded RNA."
2004	Richard Axel for the "discoveries of odorant receptors and the organization of the olfactory system."
2002	Sydney Brenner for the "discoveries concerning genetic regulation of organ development and programmed cell death."
2002	H. Robert Horvitz for the "discoveries concerning genetic regulation of organ development and programmed cell death."
2000	Paul Greengard and Eric Kandel for work in "signal transduction in the nervous system."
1998	Robert F. Furchgott for the "discoveries concerning nitric oxide as a signaling molecule in the cardiovascular system."
1997	Stanley B. Prusiner for his "discovery of Prions—a new biological principle of infection."
1994	Alfred G. Gilman and Martin Rodbell for the "discovery of G-proteins and the role of these proteins in signal transduction in cells."
1989	Harold E. Varmus for the "discovery of the cellular origin of retroviral oncogenes."

---

3   Tabulation follows that of Jewish encyclopedias.

1988	Gertrude B. Elion for the "discoveries of important principles for drug treatment."
1986	Rita Levi-Montalcini and Stanley Cohen for the "discoveries of growth factors."
1985	Michael S. Brown and Joseph. L. Goldstein for the "discoveries concerning the regulation of cholesterol metabolism."
1984	Cesar Milstein for "theories concerning the specificity in development and control of the immune system and the discovery of the principle for production of monoclonal antibodies."
1980	Baruj Benacerraf for the "discoveries concerning genetically determined structures on the cell surface that regulate immunological reactions."
1978	Daniel Nathans for the "discovery of restriction enzymes and their application to problems of molecular genetics."
1977	Andrew V. Schally for the "discoveries concerning the peptide hormone production of the brain."
1977	Rosalyn Sussman Yalow "for the development of radioimmunoassays of peptide hormones."
1976	Baruch S. Blumberg for the "discoveries concerning new mechanisms for the origin and dissemination of infectious diseases."
1975	David Baltimore and Howard M. Temin for the "discoveries concerning the interaction between tumor viruses and the genetic material of the cell."
1972	Gerald M. Edelman for the "discoveries concerning the chemical structure of antibodies."

1970	Julius Axelrod and Sir Bernard Katz for the "discoveries concerning the humeral transmitters in the nerve terminals and the mechanism for their storage, release, and inactivation."
1969	Salvador E. Luria for the "discoveries concerning the replication mechanism and the genetic structure of viruses."
1968	Marshall W. Nirenberg for the "interpretation of the genetic code and its function in protein synthesis."
1967	George Wald for the "discoveries concerning the primary physiological and chemical visual processes in the eye."
1965	Francois Jacob and Andre Lwoff for the "discoveries concerning genetic control of enzyme and virus synthesis."
1964	Konrad Bloch for the "discoveries concerning the mechanism and regulation of the cholesterol and fatty acid metabolism."
1959	Arthur Kornberg for the "discovery of the mechanisms in the biological synthesis of ribonucleic acid and deoxyribonucleic acid."
1958	Joshua Lederberg for the "discoveries concerning genetic recombination and the organization of the genetic material of bacteria."
1953	Hans Adolf Krebs for his "discovery of the citric acid cycle."
1953	Fritz Albert Lipmann for his "discovery of co-enzyme A and its importance for intermediary metabolism."
1952	Selman A. Waksman for his "discovery of streptomycin, the first antibiotic effective against tuberculosis."
1950	Tadeus Reichstein for the "discoveries relating to the hormones of the adrenal cortex, their structure and biological effects."

1947	Gerty Cori and Theresa Radnitz for the "discovery of the course of the catalytic conversion of glycogen."
1946	Hermann J. Muller for the "discovery of the production of mutations by means of X-ray irradiation."
1945	Ernst Boris Chain for the "discovery of penicillin and its curative effect in various infectious diseases."
1944	Joseph Erlanger for the "discoveries relating to the highly differentiated functions of single nerve fibers."
1936	Otto Loewi for the "discoveries relating to chemical transmission of nerve impulses."
1930	Karl Landsteiner for his "discovery of human blood groups."
1922	Otto Fritz Meyerhof for his "discovery of the fixed relationship between the consumption of oxygen and the metabolism of lactic acid in the muscle."
1914	Robert Barany for his "work on the physiology and pathology of the vestibular apparatus."
1908	Paul Ehrlich and Elie Mechnikov for their "work on immunity."

Jewish Laureates of Nobel Prize in Chemistry (27 out of 150)

2006	Roger. D. Kornberg for his "studies of the molecular basis of eukaryotic transcription."
2004	Aaron Ciechanover, Avram Hershko, and Irwin Rose for the "discovery of ubiquitin-mediated protein degradation."
2000	Alan J. Heeger for the "discovery and development of conductive polymers."
1998	Walter Kohn for his "development of the density-functional theory."

1994	George A. Olah for his "contribution to carbocation chemistry."
1992	Rudolph A. Marcus for his "contributions to the theory of electron transfer reactions in chemical systems."
1989	Sidney Altman for the "discovery of catalytic properties of RNA."
1985	Herbert A. Hauptman and Jerome Karle for the "development of direct methods for the determination of crystal structures."
1982	Aaron Klug for his "development of crystallographic electron microscopy and his structural elucidation of biologically important nucleic acid-protein complexes."
1981	Roald Hoffmann for the "theories, developed independently, concerning the course of chemical reactions."
1980	Paul Berg for his "fundamental studies of the biochemistry of nucleic acids, with particular regard to recombinant-DNA."
1980	Walter Gilbert for the "contributions concerning the determination of base sequences in nucleic acids."
1979	Herbert C. Brown for the "development of the use of boron- and phosphorus-containing compounds, respectively, into important reagents in organic synthesis."
1977	Ilya Prigogine for his "contributions to non-equilibrium thermodynamics, particularly the theory of dissipative structures."

1972	Christian B. Anfinsen for his "work on ribonuclease, especially concerning the connection between the amino acid sequence and the biologically active conformation."
1972	William H. Stein for the "contribution to the understanding of the connection between chemical structure and catalytic activity of the active center of the ribonuclease molecule."
1962	Max F. Perutz for the "studies of the structures of globular proteins."
1961	Melvin Calvin for his "research on the carbon dioxide assimilation in plants."
1943	George de Hevesy for his "work on the use of isotopes as tracers in the study of chemical processes."
1918	Fritz Haber for the "synthesis of ammonia from its elements."
1915	Richard M. Willstatter for his "research on plant pigments, especially chlorophyll."
1910	Otto Wallach for his "pioneer work in the field of alicyclic compounds."
1906	Henri Moissan for his "investigation and isolation of the element fluorine, and for the adoption in the service of science of the electric furnace called after him."
1905	J. F. W. Adolf von Baeyer for his "services in the advancement of organic chemistry and the chemical industry, through his work on organic dyes and hydro-aromatic compounds."

Jewish Nobel Prize Winners in Economics[4] (23 out of 61)

2007	Leonid Hurwicz, Eric S. Maskin, and Roger B. Myerson for "having laid the foundations of mechanism design theory."
2005	Robert J. Aumann for "having enhanced our understanding of conflict and cooperation through game-theory analysis."
2002	Daniel Kahneman for "having integrated insights from psychological research into economic science, especially concerning human judgment and decision-making under uncertainty."
2001	George A. Akerlof and Joseph E. Stiglitz for the "analyses of markets with asymmetric information."
1997	Myron S. Scholes for "a new method to determine the value of derivatives."
1994	John C. Harsanyi for the "pioneering analysis of equilibrium in the theory of non-cooperative games."
1993	Robert W. Fogel for "having renewed research in economic history by applying economic theory and quantitative methods in order to explain economic and institutional change."
1992	Gary S. Becker for "having extended the domain of microeconomic analysis to a wide range of human behavior and interaction, including nonmarket behavior."
1990	Harry M. Markowitz and Merton H. Miller for their "pioneering work in the theory of financial economics."
1987	Robert M. Solow for "his contributions to the theory of economic growth."
1985	Franco Modigliani for his "pioneering analyses of saving and of financial markets."

---

4   First prize awarded in 1969.

1980	Lawrence R. Klein for the "creation of econometric models and the application to the analysis of economic fluctuations and economic policies."
1978	Herbert A. Simon for his "pioneering research into the decision-making process within economic organizations."
1976	Milton Friedman for his "achievements in the fields of consumption analysis, monetary history and theory and for his demonstration of the complexity of stabilization policy."
1975	Leonid V. Kantorovich for the "contributions to the theory of optimum allocation of resources."
1973	Wassily Leontief for the "development of the input-output method and for its application to important economic problems."
1972	Kenneth J. Arrow for the "pioneering contributions to general economic equilibrium theory and welfare theory."
1971	Simon Kuznets, for his "empirically founded interpretation of economic growth which has led to new and deepened insight into the economic and social structure and process of development."
1970	Paul A. Samuelson for the "scientific work through which he has developed static and dynamic economic theory and actively contributed to raising the level of analysis in economic science."

Jewish Nobel Prize Winners in Physics (44 out of 176)

2005	Roy J. Glauber for his "contribution to the quantum theory of optical coherence."
2004	David J. Gross and H. David Politzer for the "discovery of asymptotic freedom in the theory of the strong interaction."

2003	Alexei A. Abrikosov and Vitaly L. Ginzburg for "pioneering contributions to the theory of superconductors and superfluids."
2000	Zhores I. Alferov for "basic work on information and communication technology."
1997	Claude Cohen-Tannoudji for "development of methods to cool and trap atoms with laser light."
1996	David M. Lee for the "discovery of superfluidity in helium-3."
1995	Martin L. Perl for "the discovery of the tau lepton."
1995	Frederick Reines for the "detection of the neutrino."
1992	Georges Charpak for his "invention and development of particle detectors, in particular the multi-wire proportional chamber."
1990	Jerome I. Friedman for the "pioneering investigations concerning deep inelastic scattering of electrons on protons and bound neutrons, which have been of essential importance for the development of the quark model in particle physics."
1988	Leon M. Lederman, Melvin Schwartz, and Jack Steinberger for the "neutrino beam method and the demonstration of the doublet structure of the leptons through the discovery of the muon neutrino."
1979	Sheldon L. Glashow and Steven Weinberg for their "contributions to the theory of the unified weak and electromagnetic interaction between elementary particles, including inter alia the prediction of the weak neutral current."
1978	Arno A. Penzias for the "discovery of cosmic microwave background radiation."

1976	Burton Richter for the "pioneering work in the discovery of a heavy elementary particle of a new kind."
1975	Ben Roy Mottelson for the "discovery of the connection between collective motion and particle motion in atomic nuclei and the development of the theory of the structure of the atomic nucleus based on this connection."
1973	Brian D. Josephson for his "theoretical predictions of the properties of a supercurrent through a tunnel barrier, in particular those phenomena which are generally known as the Josephson effects."
1972	Leon N. Cooper for the "jointly developed theory of superconductivity, usually called the BCS-theory."
1971	Dennis Gabor for his "invention and development of the holographic method."
1969	Murray Gell-Mann for his discoveries "concerning the classification of elementary particles and their interactions."
1967	Hans A. Bethe for his contributions to the "theory of nuclear reactions, especially his discoveries concerning the energy production in stars."
1965	Richard P. Feynman and Julian Schwinger for their "fundamental work in quantum electrodynamics, with deep-ploughing consequences for the physics of elementary particles."
1963	Eugene P. Wigner for his contributions to the "theory of the atomic nucleus and the elementary particles, particularly through the discovery and application of fundamental symmetry principles."
1962	Lev D. Landau for "his pioneering theories" regarding "condensed matter, especially liquid helium."

1961	Robert Hofstadter for "his pioneering studies of electron scattering in atomic nuclei" and his "discoveries concerning the structure of the nucleons."
1960	Donald A. Glaser for "the invention of the bubble chamber."
1959	Emilio Gino Segre for the "discovery of the antiproton."
1958	Il'ja M. Frank and Igor Y. Tamm for the "discovery and the interpretation of the Cherenkov effect."
1954	Max Born for his "fundamental research in quantum mechanics, especially for his statistical interpretation of the wave function."
1952	Felix Bloch for "the development of new methods for nuclear magnetic precision measurements and discoveries in connection therewith."
1945	Wolfgang Pauli for "the discovery of the Exclusion (or Pauli) Principle."
1944	Isidor Isaac Rabi for "his resonance method for recording the magnetic properties of atomic nuclei."
1943	Otto Stern for "his contribution to the development of the molecular ray method and his discovery of the magnetic moment of the proton."
1925	James Franck for "the discovery of the laws governing the impact of an electron upon an atom."
1922	Niels Bohr for "his services in the investigation of the structure of atoms and of the radiation emanating from them."
1921	Albert Einstein for "his services to Theoretical Physics" and "especially for his discovery of the law of the photoelectric effect."

1908	Gabriel Lippmann for "his method of reproducing colors photographically based on the phenomenon of interference."
1907	Albert A. Michelson for "the spectroscopic and metrological investigations carried out with his optical precision instruments."

Jewish Nobel Prize Winners in Literature (12 out of 104)

2005	Harold Pinter who in his plays "uncovers the precipice under everyday prattle and forces entry into oppression's closed rooms."
2002	Imre Kertesz, for writing that "upholds the fragile experience of the individual against the barbaric arbitrariness of history."
1991	Nadine Gordimer who through her magnificent epic writing has "in the words of Alfred Nobel—been of very great benefit to humanity."
1987	Joseph Brodsky for an all-embracing authorship "imbued with clarity of thought and poetic intensity."
1981	Elias Canetti for writings "marked by a broad outlook, a wealth of ideas and artistic power."
1978	Isaac Bashevis Singer for his "impassioned narrative art which, with roots in a Polish-Jewish cultural tradition, brings universal human conditions to life."
1976	Saul Bellow for the "human understanding and subtle analysis of contemporary culture that are combined in his work."
1966	Shmuel Yosef Agnon for his "profoundly characteristic narrative art with motifs from the life of the Jewish People."

1966	Nelly Sachs for her "outstanding lyrical and dramatic writing, which interprets Israel's destiny with touching strength."
1958	Boris L. Pasternak for his "important achievement both in contemporary lyrical poetry and in the field of the great Russian epic tradition."
1927	Henri Bergson for his "rich and vitalizing ideas and the brilliant skill with which they have been presented."
1910	Paul Heyse as a tribute to the "consummate artistry, permeated with idealism, which he has demonstrated during his long productive career as a lyric poet, dramatist, novelist, and writer of world-renowned short stories."

Jewish Nobel Prize Winners in World Peace (9 out of 95)

1995	Joseph Rotblat
1994	Shimon Peres and Yitzhak Rabin
1986	Elie Wiesel
1978	Menachem Begin
1973	Henry Kissinger
1968	Rene Cassin
1911	Alfred Fried and Tobias Michael Carel Asser

Appendix II
The Anabasis

The Anabasis is the saga of ten thousand Greek soldiers who, under Xenophon, fight their way back to their homeland after an epic retreat from the heart of Asia. Xenophon was a young Athenian civilian on the staff of the army's commanding officer. In the battle of Cunaxa, the general, hitherto victorious, was slain, and the little Greek army found itself alone and leaderless in the heart of Asia, in a strange, forbidding land teeming with enemy forces. They were cut off from food, supplies, and armaments. They did not even know the way back to their homeland. They were alone, for their leaders had gone to a parley to which the Persians had summoned them with guarantees of safe conduct. But the officers were late in returning, and soon the anxiety of their troops gave way to alarm. At last, scanning the horizon, they saw the figure of one man approaching from the distance. He was one of their own, and as they ran forward to meet him, they saw that he was badly wounded. When they reached him, he fell, and with his dying breath, he told that all the others had been treacherously murdered, and he alone had escaped.

Then began one of the most dramatic and heroic retreats ever recorded. Leaderless, the Greeks created new leaders. Slowly they began to make their way back home, under the rigid discipline of their danger and their need. The enemy harassed them from all sides. They were not even sure they knew their way back. They verged on starvation. Yet they persisted, driven forward by the yearning to return home. And one day, a roar was heard in the advanced ranks. Some in the rear thought that they had fallen into an ambush. They rushed forward but saw no enemy. They saw only their comrades, crying out in gratitude for what they saw. "The sea—the sea!" They were home.

This is truly a heroic story. An immortal story.

But ours is the story not of an army, but of an entire People, not of ten thousand but of myriads; not of a single retreat but of countless routs; not of one betrayal, but of many; not of escape across a single country, but across continent after continent; not of an ordeal lasting for months, but four thousand years. Yet even as they moved on, however remote they may have been from home, they were impelled to move on by an Inner Voice: *"Banim atem L'Adonoy*—Children are you to God."

David Polish, The Eternal Dissent (epilogue)

Appendix III
On Love and Lennon[1]

by Ze'ev Maghen

A number of years ago, I interrupted a perfectly enjoyable pilgrimage to the Old Country (the USA) in order to fly out and visit some friends in Los Angeles, that seaside sanctum of higher culture, clean air, and tasteful architecture. So there I was at LAX on a balmy Friday morning, sitting in this nondescript bar nursing a drink and waiting for my ride. Out of the corner of my eye, I absent-mindedly surveyed the vigorous maneuverings of a small but dedicated cadre of neophyte Hare Krishnas, who had deployed themselves in full court press formation across the central concourse of the airport. These mantra-chanting devotees of the swami-whose-name-I-never-could-pronounce—festooned in full-fledged religious regalia—were scurrying up and down the thoroughfare like human ping-pong balls,

---

[1] Shortened and adapted with permission from an article in Azure No. 7—Spring 5759 / 1999. My thanks to both Azure and Professor Maghen for kindly allowing me to adapt and republish this piece.

energetically hawking illustrated copies of Vedic texts to the few passersby who didn't ignore them or shove them aside.

I finished my drink and made a beeline for the exit. I guess the old quadriceps ain't quite what they used to be, though, because within seconds, I perceived a pair of dainty, be-moccasined footsteps easily gaining on me from behind. A young feminine voice inquired politely, "Excuse me, sirrr, but—ehh—maybe you vould like to take a loook at zis boook?"

I froze. Stopped dead in my tracks. I knew that accent. I'd know it anywhere. My heart plummeted into my duodenum. I put my suitcase down. I turned around slowly. She was petite and pretty in her saffron sari and multitudinous bangles. She must have had auburn hair, once, judging from the stubble on her scalp. And her eyes were a deep, feline green, amplified by the dab of yellow mustard smeared ever so artfully between them. She held a tiny tambourine in one hand, and with the other extended, was sweetly offering me a psychedelic version of the Upanishads. We stood there smack in the middle of that broad, bustling promenade and stared at each other for a few seconds, and when I saw she was about to repeat her practiced pitch about the book, I hastened to preempt and queried quietly, *"Me'eifo at?* (Where are you from?)"

"Merrramat Asharrron," she answered, naturally, effortlessly, gurgling her "r" and eliding the "h" sound as people from her neck of the coastal plains are wont to do (Ramat Hasharon is a suburb of Tel Aviv). Apparently excited by this rare opportunity to spread the Good Word in her mother tongue, she warmed to her subject, and launched into a series of sound bites concerning the benefits of Krishna consciousness, including especially the need to realize…to actualize…to visualize…to harmonize…to get in touch with…to remove the walls…to blend into…to meld…to merge…to coalesce…to become one….

I never even started listening (I know the lines by rote: I'm a frequent flyer and an erstwhile deprogrammer). *"Eich kor'im lach?"* I asked her, still trying to get my mind and heart around this. (What's your name?)

"Shira," she responded, displaying no such curiosity in return. In the meantime, the other two appropriately attired and dapperly depilated members of her Mahan squad had drifted over, no doubt intrigued by the seldom encountered phenomenon of someone actually stopping to converse, and lured by the heady scent of fresh, missionizable meat. Well, and wouldn't you know it: the whole gang is from Ramat Hasharon. Meet Ofer ("*Shalom!*") and Doron ("*Ma nishma*—what's up?").

So the four of us stand there, chatting like old friends. We reminisce about the army like good Israelis do, talk about who served where and who spent more time "in the mud" and who hated it most; Shira, as it turns out, is a first lieutenant and outranks all of us, and I snap to attention and she laughs; I remind them of this kiosk on Herzl Boulevard in Ramat Hasharon where they fry up the biggest and juiciest falafel balls in the entire country, and all three nod their heads in vehement agreement and lick their lips in almost Pavlovian recollection: they know exactly the place I'm talking about (I've never been to Ramat Hasharon, but every town in Israel has a Herzl Boulevard, and every Israeli citizen from Dan to Beersheva is convinced that there is this one falafel stand in his neighborhood that makes the biggest and juiciest falafel balls in the entire country. I saw Hawkeye do this trick on M*A*S*H once, with French-fries).

So we're shootin' the breeze, the three Hebrew Hare Krishnas and I, discoursing in the recently resurrected and unsurpassably gorgeous idiom of the biblical prophets and kings (that is, Hebrew), and finally, well, I just lose it. "What the hell are you doing here?" I blurt out, diverging slightly from the pleasantly banterish tone that has informed the conversation thus far. "You are Jews! You are Israelis, for God's sake! What the hell are you doing here, in this place, on a Friday morning, wearing these clothes, chanting those words, and selling that book?!"

Now in those days I used to read the Torah from the pulpit every week in synagogue, and since one has to rehearse continually, I never left home without the Pentateuch in my pack. At this moment, then, amazed at the extent of my own coolness, I reached back over my shoulder into my knapsack—the way I'm positive Robin Hood used to extract an arrow from his quiver—and just basically whipped out the Five Books of Moses. (Thwack!) "That's not your book," I cried, indicating the decorative and abridged Bhagavad-Gita Ofer was clutching like it was a newborn infant. "This,"—and I resoundingly slapped the raggedy, worn-and-torn volume in my own hands—"This is your book!"

They all looked at me sadly, with genuine pity, the way one might look at an animal caught in a trap or at someone who had just been diagnosed with a terminal illness. "No, no. You don't understand," purred Shira, her tone managing to be both soothing and patronizing at the same time. "This isn't a contest! We're not choosing one book over another or one religion over another; we're not expressing a preference for one culture, one nation, or one ethnic or social group over another. That would mean creating hierarchical relationships between human beings. That would mean erecting false barriers between people, barriers that have been responsible for so much misery and bloodshed throughout history, barriers that have prevented human beings from reaching their true potential and destiny, from achieving inner peace—and world peace. You and I, and everyone else in this airport, and everything that lives and breathes in every corner of this planet of ours, we are all of us part of a great and wonderful unity, we are all brothers and sisters, we are all linked by the same network of indissoluble bonds—we just don't know it yet. Krishna consciousness is about spreading that knowledge."

Zoinks! What do you get when you combine a young socialist ideologue educated in the best Israeli schools with a hefty dose of ancient Sanskrit esotericism plus a dash of the Diggers? I tried to imagine Shira haranguing conscripts in boot camp. That must have been some show.

"Look around you, *habibi* (my friend)," Doron chimed in, seemingly on cue. "The world is constantly imploding, getting smaller all the time. The distances between societies are diminishing everywhere, and the borders that divide us from one another are being erased, like a thousand Berlin Walls tumbling down. The world is progressing, moving forward, toward oneness, toward mutual tolerance and understanding, away from the petty, archaic differences that have forever pitted us against each other. As the Lord Krishna says, 'Let your hearts be as one heart, let the minds of all be as one mind, so that through the spirit of oneness you may heal the sickness of a divided community.'"

"Open your eyes!" he preached on, the already rosy cheeks of this juggernauted Jew turning increasingly sanguine with Eastern religious ardor. "These words are coming true! We are building a new reality for humankind today, and you—you are stuck, *habibi*, stuck in a past of self-isolation and limitation, hemmed in by an anachronism you refuse to let go of. But the supreme Lord Sri Krishna can help you let go of it, can help you be truly free. If you'll just concentrate and chant…"

I wondered if these guys were this good in English. Just my luck to meet up with the three most articulate initiates in the entire ashram.[2]

"Yes, you have an antiquated attitude, my friend—a dangerous attitude." This was Ofer, who was so tall that I found myself mourning his loss not just to the Jewish People as a whole, but to the Maccabee Tel Aviv basketball team in particular.

"You Are a Fascist," he proclaimed, enunciating each word with conviction and solemnity, as if he were a judge pronouncing a death sentence (that was it: No more Mr. Nice Guy. Yoga and Karma and Krishna and Swami-what's-his-name were long gone. For the moment, anyway, I was talking to pure radical Israeli leftists). "What you're preaching—it's exclusivism, it's discrimination, it's segregation, it's elitism.

"Human beings should be judged by their individual characters, not by their national or religious affiliations! Why are you so prejudiced? Why do you play favorites? What, because I was born a Jew, and that man standing over there by the telephone was not, you should interact with me in a different way than with him? Maybe he's the most upright, moral person in the entire city of LA, maybe he's calling up some charity right now to donate a million dollars!" (I glanced over at the guy. He was unquestionably Jewish, and judging from his contorted visage and wild gesticulations, was probably talking to his broker.) "And because I had the 'luck' to be born of a Jewish mother, and he didn't, for this reason you should prefer me to him? You should care about me more than you do about him? Why, that's SICK!"

---

[2] That they hadn't read the books they were so zealously peddling, and were in large degree misrepresenting Vaishnava philosophy, was clear as glass. But so what? They were declaiming the world according to themselves—and no doubt according to their Israeli parents' liberal-leaning "post-Zionist" progressivism—and that was more interesting to me, in any case. I wondered what their parents thought now…

I was glad he was done so I could stop craning my neck (remember, he was the basketball player). He might very well have been arguing as much with himself as he was with me—I hadn't managed to say very much, after all—but at any rate, Shira quickly led him aside. I wasn't getting any closer to Krishna consciousness this way. The not-so-gentle giant inhaled half the oxygen in the arrivals lounge and rattled off three mantras at breakneck speed, all in one breath. Then he was back, calm and cool, all smiles, and ready to Rama.

Shira spoke to me softly. "Don't you see? All that His Divine Grace Swami Prah...is saying comes down to this: We must strive with all our inner strength to love all people equally. That is what these books we're distributing teach as well, and, in the last analysis, isn't that also the central message of that book, the one you're carrying?" (She pointed to the Torah).

I stood there engulfed in frustration. What could I possibly answer in the few seconds remaining to us that would even begin to make a dent in all that? I heaved a long sigh of resignation. "When was the last time you read this book?" was the best I could come up with under the circumstances, appealing in all directions to imaginary back-up units.

"That's not what this book says." My ride showed up, and was of course parked in the red zone, which as you know is for the loading and unloading of passengers only. There was a genuinely poignant parting scene—during which, among other unexpected events, Doron pressed my hand and slipped me a surreptitious *"Shabbat shalom, ahi!* (Good Sabbath, my brother!)"—and the tantric trio from Tel Aviv went off in search of easier prey.

I don't know where my three semi-brainwashed but far from benighted Brahmins are now—whether they've since managed to achieve supreme bovinity, or whether they have fallen from grace and are currently putting their considerable mercantile talents to lucrative use fencing CD players on Olympic Boulevard. Either way, I sure hope I get to meet up with them again someday (yes, even if it means going back to Los Angeles). The ensuing pages contain the gist of what I would say to them, if I did.

Why Bother?

You don't have to be a disciple of Eastern mysticism or philosophy to be struck by the apparent anomaly of being a committed, involved, or practicing Jew today. You just have to be pre-lobotomy. Whatever doubts I may harbor regarding their idea of a fun Friday activity or their strange notion of musical rhythm, the objections raised by my airport interlocutors are not to be sneezed, coughed, hiccuped, or spat at. Stripped of their atavistic, pseudo-Aryan trappings and Utopian-socialist rhetoric, the positions propounded by Shira, Doron, and Ofer collectively represent far and away the foremost issue and dilemma facing the current generation of up-and-coming Jews, as they decide just how much space to give Jewishness in their lives.

For the vast majority of us, after all, the poser is not "Should I be Christian or Jewish?" or "Should I be Buddhist or Jewish?" No. The fundamental inner conflict affecting and preoccupying most of today's Jewish young people—whether formulated in this manner or otherwise—is without doubt:

Should I be a modern, progressive, secular, Westerner...or should I be actively and deeply and unabashedly Jewish—and how much of each, or where in-between? Put in even more concise fashion, the puzzle of the hour for most of us is simply this:

Why on earth be Jewish today?[3]

---

[3] An immediate qualifier: I am well aware that for a whole slew of young Jews, this issue burns inside them at about the level of a Bic lighter, if not lower. Such folks are complete strangers to the gut-wrenching inner turmoil associated with this question, and they are of two kinds. The first group doesn't think about this question because, to put it simply, they've already made their decision. Indeed, their decision was to a large extent made for them, long ago, by parents who for whatever reason did not expose their children adequately to one or the other of the two world views described above. Either the kids had religion shoved down their throats from age one—no doubts allowed (let alone cultivated)—and never really had the opportunity to observe the truly compelling aspects of life on the other side of the overly protective fence; or—what is far more common—they grew up with no exposure worth mentioning to Judaism or the Jewish People, save perhaps a few years in Hebrew school, which in the majority of cases simply furnishes the poor pupil with enduring reasons to get as far away from his cultural heritage as humanly possible. So, to you "already resolved that issue, don't bother me" types, I say: Continuous self-re-examination, even after having arrived at what appear to be immutable conclusions, is the conditio sine qua non of wisdom,

144   Why Be Jewish?

The points proffered by my three Israeli amigos are of the most profound relevance and legitimacy; they are also, of course, in no sense novel. When universities were what they should be, our collegiate predecessors were rarely known to do anything else but stay up all night in meeting halls, public parks, drinking establishments, forests, caves, and dormitories incessantly and passionately debating questions related to the epic conflict between universalism on the one hand, and particularism on the other.

Those were the days.

Not to say that the debate is dead. Over the years, I have heard the arguments of Shira, Doron, and Ofer—against attaching oneself to particularist sociocultural cliques that split humankind—advanced with conviction and passion in a whole gamut of guises by hundreds if not thousands of young Jews (not excluding, by the way, yours truly). For that matter, I suspect that many people perusing these lines right now could easily cite more than a few reasons why the notion of making the fact of their being Jewish into this big deal in their daily lives might (a) be far from compelling to them; (b) rank rather low on their priority list; (c) be entirely untenable ideologically in their view; (d) be considered just downright stupid. I know I can.

Ever since my childhood, when I was dragged to High Holiday services once a year—where my boredom was of such magnitude that it could only be alleviated by continually conjuring up the vision of myself leaping headlong from the balcony to my death by impalement on the spikes of the *menorah* below—ever since then, I remember wondering what the point of all this was. My budding bewilderment was in no way mitigated

---

humanity, meaningfulness, relationships, progress, success, and pretty much everything else worthwhile in life. So I encourage you to read on. The second group doesn't think about the question in question, primarily because (how do I put this delicately?) they don't think. Ladies and gentlemen of this mold aren't really inclined to ponder or deliberate any subjects more abstract than, say, the optimal head-height of a properly poured Heineken, the relative righteousness of the NCAA versus the NBA three-point line, how fat Oprah is this month, or what T-bills are going to do over the next quarter. Issues and ideas of identity, beauty, freedom, love, art, fantasy, justice, morality, mysticism, change, history, philosophy—such irrelevancies simply do not disturb or exercise such individuals as they pragmatically plod their way through incurably superficial lives. This piece has nothing for such folks.

by the intensely spiritual experience of my bar-mitzvah, in the course of which I learned by rote for six months how to chant flawlessly the words (although without having so much as an inkling as to their meaning) of what turned out to be the wrong *haftarah* (I kid you not). After this, I took to imbibing mass quantities of soda to help me stay up all night every night for the final month, and just barely learned the right one.

I rode a souped-up, Harley chopper right out of that neo-fundamentalist nightmare and into my carefree, suburban, red-white-and-blue American teenage dream (okay, it was a Honda). I drank, smoked, won frisbee-golf tournaments, and did everything that young people do. I was—and remain to this day—a full-blown child of Western philosophy, intent on participating in every facet of the modern universe of discourse, no holds barred. My personal nature is such that any system or institution that aspires to tell me what to do—immediately sends me fleeing for the hills, the better to organize active rebellion.

None of the above circumstances, convictions or character traits would appear at first glance to make living a full, fervent Jewish life a sensible option—let alone an attractive one—for your humble servant here. And I presume I'm not the only one in that boat.

Who Needs This?

That is the question. Why be a Jew, a committed Jew, an involved Jew, today, under current open circumstances? Why bother?

Everything logical, indeed, everything ideological in the modern, Western worldview, would appear to be solidly stacked against such a foolish stance. Inertia itself is beating us, hands and feet tied behind its back: Most Jewish young people of this relatively placid and malleable generation (the sixties it ain't) are more or less going with the conformist global flow, streaming away from everything the Jewish People once were, away from everything we could yet be together. Now that just darkens my eyes and blackens my soul, and I won't stand for it. So what comes now is basically me throwing everything I've got into one mighty attempt to convince you...to be a salmon.[4]

---

4   One last point before we embark. I am not going to advocate that we stay Jewish because

What I have to say—and the manner in which I say it—might very well offend a broad assortment of readers in a wide variety of ways (you may have already noticed this), but there's one thing I guarantee not to insult: your intelligence.

Shall we dance?

Imagine

I was in junior high school when John Lennon died, and I was an absolute wreck. I grew up on my mom's old Beatles albums, and by the time I reached adolescence, my personal classification system went: Billy Joel-John Lennon-God. So after that fruitcake son-of-a-__ emptied his revolver into this consummate musician's chest on the corner of Seventy-Second and Central Park West on the eighth of December, 1980, I wore black to school for a month. I traveled all the way to New York and waved a candle till my arm fell off and sang "all we are saying, is give peace a chance" so many times that it really was all I was saying. Meanwhile, back home, I was suspended by the principal due to an unrelated bum rap (it was Aaron Mittleman, not me, who locked our French teacher in the closet and evacuated the class), and so was conveniently able to initiate "Stay in Bed and Grow Your Hair" week—soon joined, to the principal's (and my mother's) chagrin, by some fifteen classmates—at my house in John's honor. I even went out and spent good allowance money on two Yoko albums, where she intermittently shrieks and imitates whale sounds for some eighty-five minutes straight. Now that's a true fan.

I tell you all this in order to establish my credentials as a veteran, fanatic, and peerlessly loyal Lennon lover—because now I'm going to kill him all over again.

Doron's dispensationalist vision of a new world order where there is no hatred of Jews or anybody else is pure Hindu hallucination, whereas in fact anti-Semitism will always force us to stick together in the necessary defensive formation of a persecuted clan. This may very well be the case—it has been more often than not in the past—but as a motivation, this particular claim has never been enough to get my personal motor running. I am not now and never will be a Jew and a Zionist out of fear, or because I have no choice...

John was at his best as a team player, but there's no question that his preeminent piece de resistance, the composition that will be for all time immediately associated with his name, is "Imagine." And justifiably so: I don't care what the idiot editors of Rolling Stone think, it's a great song. Gives me gargantuan goose-bumps from the introductory adagio. The man was a genius, and this was his masterpiece. Even the words themselves are enough to make you weak in the knees:

> *Imagine there's no heaven*
> *It's easy if you try*
> *No hell below us*
> *Above us only sky*
> *Imagine all the people*
> *Living for today*
> *Imagine there's no countries*
> *It isn't hard to do*
> *Nothing to kill or die for*
> *And no religion too*
> *Imagine all the people*
> *Living life in peace*
> *You may say that I'm a dreamer*
> *But I'm not the only one*
> *I hope someday you'll join us*
> *And the world will live as one*

(Tell me you didn't at least hum the melody while you were reading just now. If not, you're a freak.)

Those words, those words! They're so beautiful, so encompassing, so right. We agree with them viscerally, adopt them instinctively. They strike some of our deepest, most primal chords; they produce (at least for a moment) a kind of nebulous but heartfelt longing, a yearning for something better, for something perfect, for something beautiful. Everything we've been taught—indeed, a decent amount of what we human beings are made of—is passionately stirred by the simple yet incredibly compelling message of John's poetry.

I know what you're thinking: Oh, how predictable! Now he's going to explain how "Imagine" is just a pipe dream, an unfeasible, idyllic fantasy that's nice to sing about but has no place in our individual or collective practical planning for the future. Well, if that's what you think I'm up to…you're dead wrong.

I am not challenging the wisdom of John's enterprise because I think it has no chance of succeeding (fact is, many aspects of it are coming truer every day). If I believed in his vision, I would join up regardless, and struggle against all odds toward our common goal with all my heart, with all my soul, and with all my might.

But I don't want John's vision to be fulfilled speedily and in our days. I don't want it to be fulfilled—ever.

John's beautiful ballad is a death march, a requiem mass for the human race. His seemingly lovely lyrics constitute in truth the single most hideous and most unfortunate combination of syllables ever to be put to music. The realization of his dream, or even just a large part of it, would entail the wholesale and irreversible destruction of the dreams, hopes, happiness and very reason for living of yourself and every single person you know. If we were to live to see his wish come true, the result would be more staggeringly horrific and more devastatingly ruinous than you could ever possibly—imagine.

Although some readers have no doubt long ago reached their own conclusions on this score, permit me to share with you my own personal take on this exceedingly crucial matter.

Want Something?

Why do you get up in the morning? Please stop and think very seriously for a moment about this very significant and yet for some reason rarely broached question. What is the juice that gets you going every day? What motivates you to pursue…anything? Why, ultimately, do you do…pretty much everything you do? What are you really looking for? What have you always really been looking for?

What is the end goal, direct or indirect, of the vast majority of your activities in life? What is the one thing you need more than anything else, the one thing you just couldn't live without, the one thing you probably wouldn't want to live without? What do you live for? What do you work for? What would you die for? In the immortal words of the Spice Girls: Tell me what you want, what you really, really want....

You'll agree it's not any of the basic necessities—food, shelter, clothing, computer—you already have these. Know how I know? Because you wouldn't be reading this if you didn't. You'd be out somewhere purloining bread like Jean Valjean.

You think maybe it's your health? Look, I know that when two old Jewish men pass each other in the locker room, it's a biblical precept that at least one of them has to rasp, "If you don't have your health, you don't have nothing." Granted. But we don't live for our health. Our health is only one of the things that allow us to pursue our true desires in life. So once again: What is it, that deepest, most powerful, most true desire of ours?

"Success," you say, or "fulfillment." Okay, what on earth are those? Of what elements are they comprised, and which are their most important and indispensable component parts?

"All right—happiness!" There you go again! You've managed once more to beg the question: What is it, more than anything else, that makes you happy?

All right, here's the final clue, a Beatles clue: All you need is...

Love.

And if you think this is a cliché, then it is the single most powerful cliché ever known to humankind, the one that pervades our thoughts, directs our actions, makes us move, runs our lives. We live for love. Love of parents, love of children, love of husband, love of wife, love of sisters, love of brothers, love of family, love of friends. That's what we want and need most of all, and such a vast percentage of the things we do throughout our entire lives is ultimately connected with and geared toward achieving, maintaining, and increasing that one incomparably precious treasure: Love.

Sure, there are other objectives and experiences we may strive to attain—the fascination of scholarship, the rush of artistic creation or scientific discovery, the thrill of the fight or the game, the various physical pleasures—but tell me you wouldn't give up any of these before you'd give up love, tell me you wouldn't give up the entire kit-and-caboodle of them for the sake of love, and I'll say it again: You're a freak.

Okay, so we're agreed: no one with enough brains to read this piece will deny that love is at least one of the primary motivating factors informing human endeavor.

So let's talk just a little bit about love, shall we?

Love Your Neighbor

Two thousand years ago, they asked the famous Rabbi Akiva what his favorite verse was in the entire Bible. And wouldn't you know it, he picked "Love your neighbor as yourself," (Leviticus 19:18). A sage known as Ben-Petura said the same thing.

Now there is a fairly famous anecdote in the Talmud (Baba Metzia 62b) which describes the following situation: You and this other chap are out for a stroll in the desert. While you are both busy admiring the various lizard species and rock formations in your vicinity, he suddenly exclaims, "#@$%&! I forgot my canteen!"

You quickly assess your options. There is only enough water in your canteen for one human being to make it back to civilization alive (and no, you do not have your cell phone). So you could split the water—and you'd both perish. You could give your flask altruistically to your fellow traveler, and die a hideous death under the merciless, take-no-prisoners, desert sun. Or you could keep the canteen for yourself, and abandon him to the same fate (this is a slightly tougher decision than what shoes to wear to work in the morning). What do you do?

Two opinions, two legal rulings, are recorded in the Talmud regarding this matter. One of them comes straight from the mouth of the aforementioned Rabbi Akiva. The other one emanates from an individual known as Ben-Petura.

The scorching rays of the noonday sun are cauterizing your corpuscles, your throat is so dry you could bake a *matzah* in it, and you have quite a decision to make. Fast. Ben-Petura advises you as follows: Share the water, and die together, because you are no better than your friend. Rabbi Akiva rules differently: You keep your flask and live.

Now this is fascinating because, if you will recall, Rabbi Akiva chose "Love your neighbor as yourself" as the central message of the Bible. What is going on here? I understand Ben-Petura's position: It is entirely consistent with genuinely loving your neighbor as much as you love yourself—since I love him as much as I love myself, neither of us has any preference and I cannot possibly choose one over the other.

But what about Rabbi Akiva? What was he thinking? He put the "Love your neighbor" verse way up high on a pedestal as "the premier principle of the Torah." Yet his judgment (keep the canteen) seemed to share none of its contents. Leaving your buddy to expire miserably in the desert like a dog—seems to contradict everything that that hallowed Pentateuchal principle of mutual, equal love demands. What we have here is a clear-cut case of diametrically opposed interpretations of scriptural intention.

Ben-Petura's view was taken to an extreme by Jesus, who understands the Levitical injunction to "love your neighbor as yourself" just exactly the way it sounds (*pshuto k'mashma'o*, as we say in the holy tongue). Because you see, the entire New Testament is simply riddled with examples which leave not a shadow of a doubt that the ideal in Jesus'—and eventually Christianity's—eyes is at least to strive to love all human beings equally.

One day Jesus was in the middle of preaching to the multitudes—as was his wont—when all of a sudden (every Jewish child's nightmare), his mom showed up:

"Then one said unto him, 'Behold, thy mother and thy brethren stand without, desiring to speak with thee.' But he answered and said unto him that told him, 'Who is my mother? And who are my brethren?' And he stretched forth his hand toward his disciples, and said, 'Behold my mother and my brethren' (Matthew 12:46-49)."

This and more; Jesus wished there to be no misunderstanding regarding this matter:

"Think not that I am come to send peace on earth. I came not to send peace, but a sword. For I am come to set a man at variance against his father, and the daughter against her mother, and the daughter-in-law against her mother-in-law (Matthew 10:34-35)."

And in case it has yet to sink in:

"If any man come to me, and hate not his father, and mother, and wife, and children, and brethrens, and sisters, yea, and his own life also, he cannot be my disciple (Luke 14:26)."

We have not quoted verses out of context here. Christianity is a system concerned with belief, with faith, and as such, it recognizes no separate national entities, no tribal affiliations, not even, in the final analysis, the significance of blood kinship. It is, at least theoretically, the world's largest equal-opportunity employer, viewing as it does all human beings as similarly deserving (more accurately: similarly undeserving) potential recipients of salvation. Christianity is a thoroughly universalist—and at the same time a thoroughly individualist—religious creed, and Jesus of Nazareth was without a doubt the foremost prophet of universal love (although nowhere near the only one).

Okay, that's settled. Now, let's get married. Uh-huh, right this minute—you and me. I'm your beau of the ball, we've been having the most awesome time getting to know each other for months, and I just can't possibly wait another second. It's time to propose. Down I go on one knee. I look dreamily up into your eyes. I reach deftly into the pocket of my Giorgio Armani blazer and pull out a rock the size of a cantaloupe. I kneel before you and coo, "My darling, I love you. I love you so much. I love you as much as I love...as much as I love...as much as I love that other woman, the one walking down the street over there. See her? Oh, and that one, too, riding her bike past the newspaper stand. I love you as much as I love everybody else on this planet, and for that matter, I love you as much as I love the animals, too, and the weeds, and the plankton and—Oh God! Darling—where are you going, my daaaaarliiiiing?"

No one gets turned on by "universal" love. It doesn't get you up in the morning, it doesn't give you goose-bumps or make you feel all warm and tingly inside, it doesn't send you traipsing through fields picking wildflowers and singing songs about birds, it doesn't provoke heroism, or sacrifice, or creativity, or loyalty, or anything. In short, "universal love" isn't love at all.

Because love means preference. The kind of love that means anything, the kind of love we all really want and need and live for, the kind of love that is worth anything to anyone—that is worth everything to everyone—is love that by its very nature, by its very definition, distinguishes and prefers. Show me a guy who tells you that he loves your kids as much as he loves his own, and I'll show you someone who should never and under no circumstances be your babysitter. Stay away from such people. Head for the hills. He who aspires to love everybody the same has no idea what love means; indeed, is really advocating—and may be entirely unaware of this—the removal of all love worthy of the name from the planet Earth.

Rabbi Akiva—and classical Judaism along with him—views the matter a bit differently. The kind of love (romantic or otherwise) that he unabashedly recognizes and unreservedly encourages, is one-hundred-percent biased, hopelessly unequal, and incorrigibly preferential distinguishing love: the kind of love that plays favorites, that chooses sides, that confers specialness. As a Jewish luminary, Rabbi Akiva only understood that type of love that blossoms from the ubiquitous Hebrew root "k-d-sh," which is probably most accurately rendered into English as "to declare special, to set apart as unique."

When a man marries a woman in Judaism, the institution is called *kiddushin*, because they set one another apart from the rest of humanity, because they (ideally) love each other more than they love anybody else. When Jews bless the wine on a Friday night, this is called *kiddush*, because we are setting apart, we are distinguishing the Sabbath day from what surrounds it, and saying: I love this day more than any other day of the week.

This is not a Jewish secret. It's a human secret. It's the way we all work, all of us, deep down inside. We all love preferentially, and that's the only kind of love we value, the only kind of love we want back from the people we love. All those perpetually smiling, lovey-dovey, touchy-feely, Swami-from-Miami types who appear at first glance to be all about love, and nothing else but love, toward every single thing that lives and breathes, are in reality all about stealing this absolutely essential human emotion away from you (they've already lost it themselves). It is no coincidence that the first and most indispensable step one takes in order to successfully "deprogram" a Hare Krishna (or member of any other cult) is to rekindle his particular love for a particular someone who was once very special to him.

And this means something else that everybody already knows, but is for various reasons only occasionally acknowledged: because love is such a major deal in all of our existences, and because the love we're talking about is invariably distinguishing and preferential in nature, human beings will ever and anon, at all places and all times, prefer hanging out in the company of some people over hanging out in the company of others. They will always form special groups, little groups and big groups, groups to which they feel a special connection, a special sense of belonging. They will always relate emotionally to these groups in the manner of concentric circles, loving the nearer rings more than they love the farther ones. They will always seek to perpetuate these familial, sociocultural, and possibly political entities for as long as they can. And they will always distinguish between their own special circles, and those that are special not to them—but to others.

Is this because human beings are small-minded, visionless creatures who can't appreciate the lustrous loveliness and messianic morality of universal oneness? No. It is because they are (thank God) supremely and congenitally motivated by preferential love, and special groups of this sort are the inexorable consequence and highest, most beautiful expression of such love.

It is because loving in this way is the bread-and-butter of authentic human happiness. It is because if they didn't love in this way, human beings would have absolutely nothing left to live for. Nothing.

Do you know who nearly managed to pull off John Lennon's vision of no religions, no nations, no countries, one world—right here on earth? Do you know who almost succeeded—even if only within relative geographic and demographic microcosms—in bringing about that beautiful dream of universal love, no barriers, no walls, and no special or distinct human cliques or clans? How about these fine-feathered fellows: Stalin, Mao, Pol Pot. Any of these names ring a bell? Because the only way to stop people from loving preferentially and start them loving universally; the only way to see to it that they do not divide up—as people who love as all naturally do—into distinct sociocultural and sociopolitical communities and associations, is by forcibly ensuring that they all dress, eat, sleep, talk, sing, dance, work, play, and think the same—and killing them if they diverge. There's your "One World," John, with all the divisions and barriers erased, there's Ofer and Doron and Shira's magnificent, imploding, united utopia, where "all hearts are as one heart, all minds are as one mind, so that through the spirit of oneness you may heal the sickness of a divided community." Feast your eyes.

The Persian Carpet

My grandfather on my father's side was an Iranian Jew from a little town about a hundred and fifty miles south of Tehran, called Kashan. He told me this story.

Once, in the time of his grandfather's grandfather, already in the previous century, a Jewish merchant from Kashan allegedly overcharged a local Muslim man of the cloth. This complacent clergyman metamorphosed overnight into the Mad Mullah, and swore upon the Holy Qur'an that he'd have his revenge, and then some. He quickly assembled and whipped into a religious frenzy all the beturbaned ayatollahs in the entire province, and together they proceeded to the palace of the *qaim-maqam*, the regional governor. By hook or by crook they managed to prevail upon him to issue an official edict requiring the conversion of every single Jewish man, woman, and child to Islam by such-and-such a date, upon pain of death.

Well, the appointed deadline was fast approaching, and the Jewish community of Kashan province was in an absolute tizzy. What to do? In the end, to make a long story short, the women of the community worked like devils through day and night, scarcely pausing to rest, and made two rugs for the elders to present to the king.

Soon enough, the delegation of venerable, white-bearded old men—weary from their long trek through the desert on camel-back and donkey-back—stood trembling in His Excellency's august presence. "You have wasted your time in traveling all the way here," he chided them, right off the bat. "There is nothing that will make me change my mind. You will all be good Muslims in time for next Friday's public prayers in the mosque. Nevertheless, since you have come all this way, I will go through the motions of entertaining your petition. What have you to say?"

The elders approached the governor's divan and bowed low (real low). "Your Honor, before presenting our petition, we have brought you a gift, as a token of our gratitude for these many long years during which we have been privileged to live quietly and obediently under your powerful protection."

The governor liked gifts. Especially the kind one received from large delegations of rich and frightened Jewish merchants. "Enough of your pathetic truckling," said he. "What have you brought me?" The elders immediately had both of the carpets brought in and unfurled at the ruler's feet. "On behalf of the Jewish community of the Kashan province, we beg leave to place these two humble offerings before His Excellency, and request that he choose one of them as our tribute."

Both carpets were broad, plush, tightly woven, and made out of the most exquisite material. The first one was covered with colorful curving calyxes and designs of gold and green and turquoise, intricately intertwined with whirling waves of purple petunias, which spiraled ceaselessly and centripetally towards the median. Splendid silhouettes of every size, shape, and hue graced the corners, like an ornamental garnish surrounding and supporting a magnificent main course. The vast center was an alternately placid and surging sea of breathtaking royal blue, periodically punctuated by a cornucopia of gemlike little islands of the most elegant design, each embroidered in a different form and color and bordered by hundreds of finely interlaced, snow-white cilia swimming softly in agile and decorous understatement.

The second carpet was...red.

That's all it was. The whole rug was just one sprawling, solid red mat, from warp to woof, from end to end. "What?" cried the governor. "How dare you! I should have you all decapitated for such insolence! Do you take me for a fool? What kind of choice is this? Who in his right mind would not choose the first carpet—and who in full possession of his faculties would choose the second?"

The hoariest head of the Jewish delegation stepped forward from amongst his peers and looked the governor straight in the eye. "The silk rugs, my Liege, are the territories under your benevolent sway—Kashan province. Today that province is filled with peoples of every imaginable culture and creed—Muslims, Christians, Zoroastrians, Manicheans, Azeris, Mandeans, Turkmen, Jews—and in this way it resembles the first carpet. Would Your Excellency, then, exchange the first carpet for the second?"

"This gimmick," my grandfather would conclude with a twinkle in his eye, "plus about one hundred and seventy five thousand gold tomans placed discreetly in the governor's coffers, succeeded in averting the evil decree."

You know I have to ask: Which rug would you want? Which world do you want? The world of "Imagine," where nothing of any significance separates us, where there are "no countries and no religions," and where everybody is concomitantly possessed of the same tastes, the same loves, the same mind—where all human beings blend into one another like some kind of massive, flavorless, mud-colored milk shake?

Or would you rather the world you live in be the diametric opposite of these worlds? A world of dazzling diversity, of independent and self-respecting societies and communities that value, retain, and revel in their own uniqueness? Would you rather live in a world where real people unapologetically express real preferences for the company and society of particular persons with whom they have special cultural, historical, and emotional bonds?

Oh, when will we stop striving to be the same? We'll never get there anyway, but we'll destroy so incredibly much of what makes life interesting and mysterious and exciting and beautiful along the way. Consult your biology book. It is internal heterogeneity, which is the substance and process of human life, of all life. It is increasing variety and diversity that are the hallmark of growth, of evolution, of progress—not approaching ever nearer the great, all-encompassing One, but rather...fleeing it headlong like the plague.

Move over to psychology, and peruse your Piaget. This famous Swiss shrimp-shrink explained time and again how the deepening ability to distinguish between the self and others—and between others and others—is the most powerful indicant of infant maturation. In this manner, declared he, we go forward step by step, distancing ourselves further and further each day from our original, non-distinguishing, fetal disposition, that all-engulfing oneness which Freud dubbed "ocean consciousness."

So what is it? Is life so bad and growth so scary that you want to make a hundred-and-eighty-degree turn and head right back into the womb?

Divided we stand, my friends—united we fall.

The Global Village

"Okay," you might say, "Point taken, but it isn't exactly a new point. You're simply preaching multiculturalism. A day doesn't go by when I don't have that concept shoved in my face." Me, too, and I support it with all my heart. And I think you will agree that in order to promote and maintain authentic, polychromatic, humanity-enriching multiculturalism, we simply have to preserve and cultivate multiple, coherent, and distinctive cultures the world over. There's only one thing that the vast majority of young, fiery, and so very often Jewish advocates of the modern multicultural approach almost always seem to forget: that one of the foremost examples of such cultures is their own.

What kind of sense does it make when (among others) college-age, Jewish-born intellectuals espouse the toleration, nay, celebration of the international cultural mosaic, while at the same time entirely ignoring and neglecting almost everything even remotely Mosaic? Is it not astounding—along similar lines—that the same Jewish postmodernist professors who have for three decades and more decried "Western Cultural Imperialism" of every type, are in the overwhelming majority of cases themselves the very personification of the unconditional surrender of what is perhaps the most ancient and enduring non-Western culture—their own Jewishness—at the feet of that very same

"Western Cultural Imperialism?" What is going on in the hearts and heads of Jewish students who ostensibly support constructive dialogue and illuminating interaction among different ethnic, national, cultural and religious groups—but identify only peripherally (if at all) with their own? How on earth can people be expected to tolerate, respect, and eventually learn from each other's sociocultural differences...if they don't have any?

The Global Village is getting me down. I buy an outrageously expensive airline ticket, board the plane in New York, and squirm around uncomfortably in my chair for ten hours; the bird lands, I deplane and, lo and behold, I'm right back where I started from: the same English language plastered all over the storefronts, the same Calvin Klein jeans plastered on everybody's behind, the same pop music as back in the States issuing ever so rhythmically from the taxi driver's radio (though neither he nor his passengers could ever possibly decipher a word of it—which, by the way, makes them very lucky people, if you ask me). Why are so many people driven by this lukewarm, lemming-like, perennial search for sameness? Why don't they prefer being themselves—both individually and collectively?

Am I advocating that nations and cultures insulate themselves, that they dig in behind an ethnocentric and xenophobic fortress and erect all types of intellectual and ideological tariffs, the better to maintain their separate group identity, their "cultural purity?"

Not on your life. Au contraire! I am specifically and passionately advocating that the various sociocultural units of the world interact and share, that they challenge, stimulate, edify, surprise, enlighten, influence, and open the eyes of one another.

But in order to share, you have to have what to share, you have to cultivate, and become knowledgeable about, and rejoice in, and build upon your own unique, accumulated heritage. You need to cherish and nourish specifically the distinguishing traits and characteristics that make you different and fascinating, and place you in possession of tantalizing and desirable gifts to bestow upon others—things they don't already have! (Who wants to bring home a Bruce Lee or Michael Jackson T-shirt as a souvenir from Morocco? And yet these were the only two examples of Moroccan fashion memorabilia available at the Abu'l Hadi and Sons souvenir shop in Fez when I was there.) If you sow rutabaga and I grow kumquats, we certainly have every impetus to trade with each another; if we both plant kidney beans—what's the point?

I guess like most people, my general ideas about "the way things should be" are to a large extent the product of my childhood. My suburban Philadelphia block was made up of about ten separate houses with ample space between, all of which formed the peripheral ring around this huge, green, common lawn in the middle. The families inhabiting these houses—the Ciartes, the Fitzgeralds, the Popowitches, the Hing-Yips, the Rosenbergs, the Sanchezes—were as incurably and pridefully diverse as the architecture of the houses themselves. Visiting each other, as we often did, was a mind-expanding tour de force: the unexpected smells, the strange conventions, the vastly different notions of decor (for years I begged my parents to paint the inside of our house pink and green like the Ciartes had).

Now, what if someone had taken all these families, and somehow convinced them that it was a waste of space, all these separate houses; a waste of crockery, all these diverse dishes; a waste of artistic effort, all these varying internal and external decors? Everybody should move into one big, humongous house and do all that stuff together, and uniformly. Then everything would be hunky-dory, and far more economical, and look how much closer and more unified everybody would be!

How would you like to live in that house?

We need our separate houses. It's the only way we can be good neighbors. It's the only way we can avoid butchering each other with chainsaws and Ginsu knives in a matter of two to three days, tops. And it's the only way that the interaction between us—nightly on the grassy knoll, or daily in the world of work—can bear any fruit and be any fun. Just as you no doubt live your personal life within a given community as an individual, self-confidently sporting your own singular and special trademark qualities, so nations and ethnic groups need to actively participate in and contribute to the world order and the totality of human civilization as proud, particular, peculiar, unique sociocultural entities, each boasting a brash and defiant attitude of "national individualism," each, as it were, building, decorating, and living in its own distinctive cultural home within the overall neighborhood of nations.

"Gotcha!" you say, a self-satisfied smirk spreading speedily across your visage. "By your logic, then, we should none of us affiliate with any association or community or nation or even family. Rather, we should focus solely on our own, independent, individual selves—renouncing loyalty to or prejudicial affection for any one particular group—and thereby provide the world with the largest amount of variety and individualism possible! Six billion different and unique colors!"

This is indeed the conclusion which has been reached, consciously or unconsciously, by a great many members of what is often (correctly) referred to as "alienated Western society." But if you love everybody you love nobody—and if you love nobody you love nobody. It's a big circle, and you've come full 'round it. You're talking about eradicating preferential love again—or at least severely restricting its scope and outlets to yourself and perhaps a few intimate relatives and acquaintances (is that all the love you've got?). You are talking about opting out of having a special community.

And consider, if you will, the humble Persian carpet from my grandfather's story. Suppose the elders of Kashan had unrolled before the governor not two rugs, but three: the first of elaborate and colorful design, as described; the second, just plain red; and the third, made up of literally tens of thousands of tiny pixels and knots, each dyed its own unique tint, and with no attempt at thematic organization or color coordination whatsoever. What would that rug look like? Dreck, that's what. Neither full-blown universalism nor full-blown individualism makes for a beautiful world. Only a world that is based on a conception and structure planted firmly between these two poles can ever be called truly beautiful.

For God's sake, be an individual—and an individualist! I for one certainly lay claim to such a title—with a vengeance. It is because I know that nobody can ever take my "me-ness" away from me without a sawed-off twelve-gauge shotgun—it is because of this that it never occurred to me to be afraid that I would lose myself in a crowd; it is because of this that I am able and willing to provide myself with the incredible privilege of being an integral participant in that unparalleled, nearly impossible phenomenon...called the Jewish People.

Unlike most (all?) other religions, we Jews are members of an extended family, of a Nation, and of a "Tribe." We have never referred to ourselves anywhere in our sources as *"dat Yisra'el"* (the Religion of Israel) or *"emunat Yisra'el"* (the Faith of Israel). Rather, we have always denoted ourselves throughout our long history by the significant cognomens *"am Yisra'el"* (the Nation of Israel), *"klal Yisra'el"* (the Totality of Israel), *"knesset Yisra'el"* (the Assembly of Israel), *"beit Yisra'el"* (the House of Israel) and *"bene Yisra'el"* (the Children of Israel). You see where the emphasis lies, right?

War and Peace

A few issues, however, may still be troubling you. For instance: isn't the world I am asking for perforce a world forever doomed to incessant, desolating warfare between peoples, all of whom love "their own" with a passion and hate everybody else with the same?

For starters, even assuming the One-Worlders could ever bring us peace, which they most definitively cannot, it would only be at the price of a terrorist, totalitarian, socially engineered nightmare worse than those of George Orwell and Aldous Huxley. That is the only possible, earth-bound consummation of the words, "Imagine all the people, living life in peace." (Stop humming.) If you've got no will, no emotions, no preferences and no special ties left to speak of, I guess that'll take the fight out of you pretty good, all right.

Contrary to the patriotic idea that "it is good to die for our country"—you would probably agree with me that there isn't the slightest thing good about dying for your country, your nation, your religious beliefs, or whatever. I don't wish this fate upon anybody. What I do wish, upon every single person still persevering through these pages, is that you do have things in your life that are dear enough to you that you would be willing to die for them, if it ever—God forbid—became absolutely necessary. Says John: "Nothing to kill or die for...." Says me: In that case, nothing much to live for, either.

Emotional Transference

There is another important subject to be addressed in this connection, however, a subject we left dangling more than ten pages ago. Back then we were trying to figure out the motives of Rabbi Akiva for apparently contradicting himself by lauding the precept "love your neighbor as yourself," while at the same time ruling elsewhere (in the case of the flask of water in the desert) that when it comes to choosing between your life and that of your neighbor—your life is paramount. We have tried to show that as a Judaic scholar, Rabbi Akiva was reared on the principle of preferential love, and thus he ruled as he did. But we still haven't resolved the seeming disagreement between his ruling and the explicit scriptural prescription he praises so highly. Let's try to do that now.

Last week I was sitting in this Yemenite restaurant in Jerusalem reading a book and enjoying the cultural cuisine. At seven p.m., the news came on and the anchorperson announced that two hundred thirty people had been killed in an airplane crash in Indonesia.

"That's terrible," I thought, and proceeded to cut myself another large, juicy morsel of delicious Yemenite food and loft it lazily into my watering, hangar-like mouth. Yummmmm. "That's really awful—oh, there's a nice big piece of chicken smothered in delectable spicy sauce; come to papa...mmmm, yummmm...."

And then I stopped. I was actually a little angry at myself for being unable to get sufficiently upset about those two hundred thirty Indonesians and their poor, grief-stricken, destroyed families to have it affect my appetite even for five seconds. So I tried an experiment. I took the headline I had just heard on the radio, and changed only one or two words. Now it read: Two Hundred Thirty Israeli Soldiers Die in Plane Crash over Negev Desert.

"Oh, God. That really hurts. It physically hurts. As if someone punched me really hard in the stomach. Is that what it feels like? That much pain? I'm not thinking about my next bite of food anymore, that's for sure. I'm pretty close to being nauseous. So now I know. Now I have some inkling at least of what those crushed, devastated, wrecked, innocent families are experiencing right now, as the news reaches them one by one that everything they ever lived for is gone. Dear God...."

You may not believe this, but I actually got up and left without finishing my food (and there was at least a third still sitting there on the plate). I know, I know: my momentary abstinence really helped those Indonesian families. That's not my point. Let me give you another example.

A couple of years ago I was under Manhattan, riding the One Train downtown to South Ferry. Round about Sixty-Sixth Street, the door on the end of our car slid open, and a man with no legs came through, propelling himself with his arms and carrying a bucket in his teeth. He didn't say anything (obviously), wore no explanatory sign, but I guarantee you this: by the time he made it to the other end of the car, there were easily upwards of fifty more dollars in that bucket. Granted, people give for all types of reasons. But I know what made me at least reach for the paper and not the change. It wasn't "altruism," whatever that is. It was really a much simpler, more compelling deal: as I would imagine most other people did on that train, I looked at that indescribably miserable man and instinctively said to myself, "My God: what if that were me? What if that was my father, or my brother, or my son?"

Preferential love is the most powerful love there is, the only truly motivating love there is. It is by means of that love—the special love we harbor for those close to us—that we learn how to begin to love others, who are farther away. Genuine and galvanizing empathy for "the other" is acquired most effectively and lastingly through a process which involves, first and foremost, immersion in love of self, then of family, then of friends, then of community...and so on. It is via emotional analogy to these types of strong-bond affections that one becomes capable of executing a sort of "love leap," a hyperspace transference of the strength and immediacy of the feelings one retains for his favorite people, smack onto those who have no direct claim on such sentiments.

If you don't love your own best of all, we said, you really have no idea what genuine love is. If you have no idea what genuine love is, your chances of learning to love people in Indonesia or Syria or Tajikestan or Wyoming, your chances of learning to feel for people in faraway places or contexts (or on the other side of a tense border, or in the opposite camp of a kulturkampf), are pretty slim indeed.

Here, then, is (my guess at) Rabbi Akiva's exegesis of the much-touted verse, "Love your neighbor as yourself." In his eyes, it doesn't signify "love your neighbor as much as you love yourself"; Rabbi Akiva doesn't believe in such artificial love, we know that from the flask story. To him it reads (and the Hebrew happens to support this): "Love your neighbor in the same fashion as you love yourself." Use the feelings you have toward yourself as a guide for how to feel about him. You will never love him as much as you love yourself—you *should* never love him as much as you love yourself—but you will learn to love him at all, in the first place, solely through your overwhelmingly powerful love of yourself and your own. It is to this process and no other that the Torah refers when it urges—in over twenty different versions of the same statement—"Love the stranger, for you were strangers in the land of Egypt (Deuteronomy 10:19)."

The world of preferential love and distinct ethnic, social, and cultural and political entities certainly need not be one of hatred and interminable warfare (What is Isaiah's vision? "Nation shall not lift up sword against nation, neither shall they learn war anymore [Isaiah 2:4]"). It may, in fact, be the only system available to the human race that will ever have a chance of breeding genuine global empathy and tolerance.

Imagine that.

Why Choose the Jews?

You are still not happy. "Okay," you might say, "I'll concede, for the moment, the following points: (1) I accept that the kind of love that means the most to me is preferential, distinguishing love: I want it, I need it, I can't live without it; (2) I'll give you that the world should optimally resemble a tapestry of distinctive families, or groups, or peoples, or nations; and (3) I'll even grant you that I personally, for the sake of my own happiness and for the general good of humanity, should connect myself in a vigorous and loving fashion to one of said groups. Fine. What you haven't really told me is...why on earth should that group be the Jews?"

Well said. After all, you might claim that you've had little or no exposure to Judaism or the Jewish community, so what's it to you; or you might claim that what meager exposure you did have was not exactly tantalizing, and you can't see much point in going back for seconds; or you might (finally) ask this extremely excellent question: Why shouldn't I adopt as my "special society" all the members of the intramural hockey league I play in? Or all the guys I go bowling with? Or all the people who live in the same city I do? Or all the people who live in the same country I do (I'm as good a patriot as the next fellow!)? Why not these groups as my first love? After all, some young Jews have more in common with non-Jews than your average Jewish person walking down the street.

Here the tone needs to change. Because here we stand on the threshold of things that often belong to emotion. And it is very hard—indeed, well nigh impossible—to logically argue something that belongs to the kingdom of the heart. Nevertheless, I'll give it my best shot.

I could start by telling you how much we need you, and how much what you personally decide to do with your life has earth-shattering consequences and ramifications for your whole extended national clan, wherever they sleep and dream, wherever they wake and work, wherever they fight and fall. Jewish tradition tells this terse tale: There are twelve people in a boat. One guy, he starts drilling a hole under his seat. When everybody gapes at him in dismay and astonishment, he looks up and says, "What's it to ya? I'm only drilling under my own seat."

The idea is, of course, that we Jews are all in the same boat, so your particular actions or inactions naturally attract our interest and concern, whether you like it or not—because they are inextricably bound up with our collective prospects and welfare. Make no mistake about it: whether you are aware of this or not, the future of the Jewish People is as much up to you as it is up to the Israeli Prime Minister. But this is too close to a Jewish guilt trip, and I'm just not into that.

I could also advance the proposition that you ought to join us with a passion and a fury for the following very simple reason: You are a Jew. You are a Jew, and another Jew (who was once upon a time extremely assimilated)—the founder of the modern State of Israel once declared plainly, "The greatest happiness in life, is to be that which one is." I couldn't agree more. And if you are going to be who you are—a Jew—then do it up. Don't be a "by-default Jew," a "checkbook Jew," a "High-Holiday Jew," a "peripheral Jew" or a "marginal Jew." Be a "bold, breathless Jew," be a "wild, wanton Jew," be an "I'm going to milk this cultural identity thing for everything it's got Jew"—be a knowledgeable, thirsty, caring, daring, actively involved Jew.

This approach answers the whole question for some Jews but you may simply claim that "being who you are" at this point in your life entails being a bowler, or a feminist, or a Bostonian, or an American or Canadian, far more than it does being a Jew, which is "what you are" only due to an accident of birth. There are various approaches and I'd like now to share mine. Again, the gnawing question: "Why not choose my bowling buddies, or the people on my block, or the International Society of Vegans, or who knows what other coherent entity as my spiritual center and the object of my primary affections? Why is the Jewish People a better candidate for this exalted position in my thoughts and emotions than these previously named options?"

Let's hum along with Dr. Winston O'Boogie—Lennon's favorite nickname—once again: "Imagine all the people, living for today...." Living for today. Oh, John, my main man, what is it? Did you think about this wish before you made it? Granted, this line suffers a number of possible interpretations, but they all more or less connect to the problem I would like to raise here.

We have already discussed the ugliness and emptiness engendered by the modern Western ailment of exaggerated individualism and complete non-affiliation. Well, one thing is for sure: being Jewish cures this affliction, like no antidote I've ever seen. As a Jew, you literally have millions of people all around you, right this very second, throughout the world, with whom you share a secret, with whom you can exchange a knowing glance, at whom you can wink (use your judgment). These people are your people, they feel tied to you, they are pulling for you, they are on your side (travel tip: this does not mean you will not get ripped off by Israeli cab drivers—that's their way of saying, "I love you").

I don't know if this special relationship is a product of the historical and international uniqueness of the Jewish phenomenon—we are neither a "nation" like the French, nor a "religion" like the Christians—or whether it is because as a group, we are not too big (like the population of America) and not too small (like the tenants in your apartment building), but just the right size to elicit that super-family feel, that combination of transcendence and immanence, of greatness and closeness. Or maybe it is just because the rest of humanity has always been so kind to us. I don't know exactly why there is this powerful electricity constantly coursing and pulsating between Jews the world over—I just know it's there.

Just before my latest stint in the reserves, I was in New York blading with my brother down the lower West Side promenade hard by the Hudson, and we stopped to rest near the World Trade Center. Alex and I switched to Hebrew in order to have some privacy and, as we were talking, this be-suited fellow sitting on the bench opposite—clearly taking a five-minute lunch break from an action-packed morning of corporate raiding—kept staring at us. Finally, he rose, walked over, and stood rather awkwardly dead center in front of our bench. I looked up at him, and he faltered, gestured, fumbled, hesitated, and then just stammered, "Um...uh...Shalom!" I extended my hand and he shook it warmly and smiled. Still flustered, he half-saluted us goodbye, and went back to merging and acquiring.

What he really wanted to say was, "Hey—I'm Jewish, too." What he really intended by "Um...uh...Shalom," was, "I embrace you, my brother, member of my Tribe from a faraway place. We share something tremendous and indescribable, something ancient and exalted, something wonderful and mysterious. We were soldered together, you and I, by the fires of hell on earth, and our bonds are since unsunderable. I'm glad you are in the world, and it gives me strength and pleasure to see you. Here: have some genuine affection." He meant all this, and more. He wanted to momentarily close that circuit and tap into that energy flow.

The modern Western sickness of living solely for oneself, however—for which Jewish identity is such a powerful serum—is usually accompanied by another malady, which Lennon and so many others aspire to infect us all with: living solely for today. This second disorder—let's call it "time hermitism," for lack of a better term (is there a worse term?)—emaciates our psyches by disconnecting us from a vast and fascinating potpourri of mind—and soul—expanding elements on the vertical—or temporal—plane. You can be alone in space, and you can be alone in time.

"Living for today"—an extremely pervasive slogan among so many people for so many years—means, essentially, being alone in time, alone historically speaking (a feat which can obviously be achieved even while surrounded in the present by a whole soccer stadium's worth of companions). Well, I suppose that's fine, if that's what you like. Living for the moment—and only for the moment—has certain genuine advantages. But I think that in the long run, you lose out big time. I mean, let's reason from the specific to the general again: did you ever see that Star Trek where they strap Kirk down into a big, black, padded chair, and beam this memory-erasing light at his head, such that after a few minutes he would have been emptied of all recollection? Now suppose we strapped you into that chair, and erased your entire memory—everything you did, everything you felt, everything you learned, everything you treasured, everything to which you daily and constantly referred. What, do you suppose, would be left?

A turnip, that's what. "You" are the accumulation of your experiences throughout your life. Growing and living and enjoying and fulfilling is all about the interaction, combination, and application of those past experiences—which constitute the greater part (if not the whole) of your consciousness—to what it is you are thinking, feeling and doing at the present instant. If all you know and all you feel is what you know and feel today—or this week, or this year—well, you aren't going to get invited to a lot of dinner parties, I can promise you that.

But along the same lines, "you" are—or should be—even more. Why settle, after all? You have the opportunity to extend your horizons further than any normal eye can see, further than any detached intellect can perceive, further than any untouched heart can feel. You can reach beyond your individual, birth-and-death-bound walls, and palpate immortality. You can draw on, you can gorge upon, the accumulated experience, knowledge, and inextinguishable fire of the manifold ascending centuries that preceded you. You can stand higher than Everest on the shoulders of a hundred generations, and thereby see light-years farther into the future than those who have grounded themselves at sea level, and cannot see past their noses in any direction. In a word: you can be HUGE.

How does one do all this? After all, you personally were born quite recently. You haven't existed, built, climbed, fallen, lost, won, wept, rejoiced, created, learned, argued, loved, and struggled for thousands of years. Nevertheless, you happen to have lucked out. As a Jew, you are a distinguished member of a Nation that has done all these things, and then some. You have special eyes, eyes that can see for miles and miles. If you only will it, you can extend your arms and touch the eons and the millennia, you can suck in the insights and bask in the glory and writhe in the pain and draw on the power emanating from every era and every episode and every experience of your indomitable, indestructible, obstinately everlasting People.

This is not an ability acquired solely through learning or reading (although this is a major ingredient, I hasten to emphasize); it is first and foremost a function of connection, of belonging, of powerful love. If you reach out and grasp your people's hands—you were there. You participated in what they did, in all places at all times; you fought their battles, felt their feelings, and learned their lessons. You tended flocks with Rachel, and slaved in Potiphar's house with Joseph; you sang in the wilderness with Miriam, and toppled the walls of Jericho with Joshua; you carried first fruits to the Temple Mount, and were mesmerized by Elijah on the slopes of Carmel; you brought the house down on the Philistines with Samson; you fought the chariots of Hatzor under Deborah, and danced before the ascending Ark with David; you went into exile with the prophet Jeremiah, and hung your harp and wept by the rivers of Babylon; you defied the divinity of Nebuchadnezzar with the courage and cunning of Daniel, and vanquished the might of imperial Persia with the wisdom and beauty of Esther; you sought communion with the infinite with Shim'on bar Yohai, and studied law and lore in the vineyards of Yavneh with El'azar ben Arach; you were with Judah the Maccabee at the first Chanukah, with Rabbi Akiva in the Roman torture chamber and with Bar-Kochva in Betar; you devoted your life to Torah in Babylon, and learned Torah and philosophy by the Nile with the students of Maimonides; you were crucified for refusing to convert in the Crusades; you were exiled from the shores of Spain by Isabella; you went out dressed in white to Tsfat's fields to greet the Sabbath bride with Rabbi Isaac Luria, and went into Galicia's huts to seek the ecstasy of the fervent Ba'al Shem Tov; you fled the Black Hundreds across Russia's taiga, and were welcomed by Emma Lazarus at the gates of Ellis Island; you filed into gas chambers at Bergen Belsen; you parachuted into Hungary with Hanna Senesh, and fought back at Warsaw with Mordechai Anilewitz; you were shot with your family in the forests of Poland, and dug a mass grave and perished there at Babi Yar; you revived your dead language, you resurrected your sapped strength, you returned to yourself and your ancient country; you rebuilt and you thrived.

I am a Jew, and I am tied to teleology as well as to history. I live not just "for today," and not even just for all that has led up to today—I also live for a thousand tomorrows. I do not know what will be in ten centuries from now, but I know that Jews will be. How do I know? Because I will work for it, because I will see to it—and I believe in myself as much as I believe in my People. Yes, Jews there will be. And through them, I will be, and through them, I will touch what will be, and through them, I will create what will be.

You and I are members of a unique, extended family, extended in time as well as in space, extended into the future as well as into the past. My noble ancestors will pardon me for the odious comparison, but it is like having access to a vast internet of Existence, like being plugged-in and logged-on to forever (and believe it or not, at the highest and deepest levels, the connection is interactive). In the words of Leo Tolstoy (not that we need his approval or reinforcement, he just happens to be the world's most talented writer, and he put this—and everything else—rather nicely):

> *The Jew is the emblem of eternity. He whom neither slaughter nor torture of thousands of years could destroy, he whom neither fire nor swords nor inquisition was able to wipe off the*

> *face of the earth, he who was the first to produce the oracles of God, he who has been for so long the guardian of prophecy, the pioneer of liberty and the creator of true civilization, and who transmitted all these to the rest of the world—such a Nation cannot be destroyed. The Jew is as everlasting as eternity itself.*

You need not, then, live the impoverished life of the "time hermit." You, my sister or brother, spiritual daughter or son of Sarah and Abraham, you are blessed with the opportunity to connect with and benefit from a sprawling, boundless, spatial, and temporal network, suffused with the deepest secrets of the ages, humming with the love of countless generations, a love that was always channeled directly and unhesitatingly at you.

By tying into all of this—while fiercely maintaining your own, stubborn individuality—you indeed achieve a great deal: you add innumerable new intellectual and emotional dimensions to your life, as you absorb, meltdown, and refashion in your own image the fruits of untold centuries of evolving Jewish thought and churning Jewish tumult; you teach yourself the syntax and vocabulary of a timeless language, which you can use—as it were—to communicate with all that went into creating you, and all that you will one day create; you partake in a four-thousand-year-long journey of savage struggle and jubilant exultation, of unimaginable sacrifice and ineffable beauty, an adventure recently rekindled in a phoenix-like flash of incandescent splendor the likes of which human history has never seen; and eventually you burn, my brother and sister, you burn with the light and the fever and the strength and the passion of the magnificent and undying People of Israel, the bush that burns, but is never consumed.

Try getting that from bowling.

Dr. Ze'ev Maghen is the Chair of The Department of Middle Eastern History at Bar-Ilan University in Israel and a research associate at the Begin-Sadat Center for Strategic Studies.

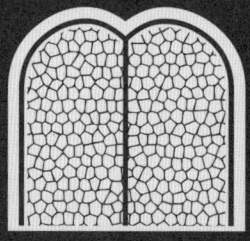

MOSAICA PRESS
BOOK PUBLISHERS
Elegant, Meaningful & Bold

info@MosaicaPress.com
www.MosaicaPress.com

The Mosaica Press team of acclaimed editors and designers is attracting some of the most compelling thinkers and teachers in the Jewish community today. Our books are available around the world.

HARAV YAACOV HABER
RABBI DORON KORNBLUTH